# Sporting the Right Attitude

## Lessons Learned In A Troubled Family

Walter Jackson, Msc.D.

Cover Design by Cathi Stevenson


ISBN 0-9634086-3-1



Manufactured in the United States of America

1ST Printing, Soft Cover

Published by
SELF AWARENESS TRAININGS, LLC
645 West 9th Street, Unit 110
Los Angeles, California 90015-1640
Los Angeles, California 90027

# Dedication

This book is dedicated to my belated parents, Walter and Dorothy Jackson, who did the best they could raising our family; to my children, Ryan, Devon and Jasmine who have brought much love and joy to my life; my mother-in-law, Evelyn Benton who has always been there to support the family; and others mentioned throughout this book whose lives have touched mine in their own unique way, and to the reader for whom I hope this book will provide awareness, inspiration and understanding.

# Special Thanks

Special thanks to my editor Maggie Frost. To my soul mate, my wife Janet, for her priceless gifts of understanding, caring and support...as well as the long hours helping me research, and her invaluable editorial assistance.

# Table of Contents

# Preface

During the time it has taken to write this book, I have been content with the title "Sporting the Right Attitude." Sports allowed me to taste the fruits of victory as I won games early in life. Sports also helped me survive growing up in a violent family.

Let me explain what I mean. As a child, I was under pressure, but I didn't know how to handle my anger, my hurt, and all of the other negative emotions that surfaced in me. It was sports that helped me most to direct my thoughts positively.

I focused on athletics because sports have assumed such a predominant position in our society over the past four decades. The television industry has increased its sports programming time because public interest has grown — or could it be the other way around?

Media coverage has allowed us to follow our favorite teams or athletes from training right up to their final games. Games have become faster and talent more abundant, forcing today's athletes to be even more versatile. Over time, the top athletes are increasingly stronger, taller and faster than their predecessors. Similarly, world records continue to be broken again and again. Nevertheless, one essential quality successful athletes need, remains the same: the right attitude.

Athletes know that in order to win, they must maintain winning thoughts regardless of the adversities they may face.

Just as the athlete must have the right attitude in order to win the game, anyone, with the right attitude, can cope with the emotional stresses of their troubled family.

The skills I developed in sports, along with the courage and principles I later discovered, taught me that we can have inner peace while the outer world appears to be falling apart. Sense of confidence is built up through sports — a reassurance that somehow things will always turn out all right as long as you do your best.

I was certain I would be able to escape my family violence if I received an athletic scholarship. Several universities had expressed an interest in my athletic ability in football, basketball and track during my junior year in high school. But I watched my dream of becoming a professional athlete slip away when I was injured in a car accident that left me in a coma for three days, and took my best friend's life.

The road back to physical and mental recovery was a difficult one. I now realize that I suffered emotionally because at the time I had no knowledge of certain principles that I am sharing with you in this book.

Many athletes use practical methods to rise to a higher consciousness to help them overcome challenges on and off the playing field. By using constructive channels of thought, most athletes learn to believe they are winners. Coaches use helpful principles such as visualizations, affirmations, mindfulness, and pep talks to inspire their players to believe in themselves, to realize and achieve their greatest potential.

In the world of sports, as well as in normal day-to-day activities, people need to further their own spiritual awareness, to believe in the rightness of what they do. Somehow, spiritual power magically and effortlessly brings us to an inner peace.

But it's impossible to be enthusiastic about our own lives if others — family members, peers, co-workers, supervisors — are allowed to control us with negative attitudes. When we give our power away to someone else, we are bound to stumble. However, people who trust themselves will succeed.

I ran into many psychological brick walls and spent years trying to find my way, until I realized that what I was really searching for was inner peace. The answers I was seeking were being constantly whispered into my ear by my inner self.

My greatest fulfillment was learning that there is a greater power within us that can provide an inner peace and won't let us fail if we keep believing. We can learn how to nurture and channel this power. Whatever we call it — self-acceptance, inner light, the voice of God — the power of belief will surface to help us win.

Nothing is more important in the journey of life than to gain an understanding of our individual power, to unify with it, and to become empowered. Many famous athletes who are considered physical supermen and superwomen and who have performed outstanding feats have been able to do so because they have become partners with that inner power.

So can we.

Yes, this is the good news — that people can learn, and they can change their reality by changing their attitudes.

# Sporting the Right Attitude

## Lessons Learned In A Troubled Family

A*cknowledge*

T*he*

T*ruth*

I*nvestigate*

T*he*

U*nknown*

D*eclare*

E*xcellence*

## CHAPTER 1

# Family Blueprints

*"You have no idea what a poor opinion I have of myself and how little I deserve it."*

W.S. Gilbert

A lot of single-parent families lived in the government housing project where I grew up in Stockton, California. My household was one of only a few where both parents lived at home.

Although my parents physically fought often, I felt fortunate to have both of them living in the same household, despite the shame and embarrassment they caused me with their constant fighting. I frequently heard people gossiping about my parents, saying they fought like "cats and dogs."

I was ashamed because it seemed that all my friends in the project knew about our dysfunctional family. I tried to justify my feelings by telling myself that my parents' fighting was acceptable behavior since they both lived at home. Most of my friends only had one parent at home.

I carried a tremendous amount of anger and fear, but I didn't understand why. These feelings made me confused about myself and others.

Whenever a situation arose that triggered these insecure emotions, I would blame anyone and everyone in trying to defend myself. Not once did I try to figure out why I was so insecure. I even began to believe that maybe I was to blame for the family's problems.

My father, who was a very quiet person, kept his feelings bottled up inside and would seldom talk. I never saw my parents discuss their problems. They would simply argue. It seemed that arguments and physical fights were the only ways they could deal with their differences.

One summer, my father's brother, Charles Jackson — who had enlisted in the United States Army and was stationed in Germany — came to see us. He had received new orders that stationed him in San Francisco, 90 miles away. Charles felt this would be an ideal opportunity to visit his brother and family, whom he had not seen in almost eight years.

On Uncle Charles' last visit, I was two years old. But now I was 10, old enough to feel my father's excitement. He very seldom showed his joy, but I could sense his happiness this day.

I was at school that morning when my father picked up his brother at the Greyhound bus station. My parents knew sports were dear to my heart, so even though Uncle Charles was coming, they allowed me to stop off at the gym in the projects after school to practice with the community basketball team.

After practice I headed for home. As I walked along, I felt good, I felt talented and special, full of confidence to tackle life's challenges. I needed sports for escape. I felt my life depended on football, basketball, baseball and track and field in more ways than one.

When I arrived home, Uncle Charles was sitting on the couch in the living room. He gave me an affectionate hug and sat down to talk warmly with me about things I was interested in. I would have liked to experience this affection from my parents but they did not feel the freedom within themselves to take each other's hand or kiss in front of their children. It seemed they could not get past their negative emotions.

I thought how nice it was to know your blood relatives — maybe because it would seem easier to share my genuine feelings with a relative than with my parents. I wanted to express those feelings that had been knotted up inside me for years.

I had come to believe our relatives who lived out of state didn't like our family. They would usually visit other relatives in California, but never seemed to have time to come to Stockton. I felt that, except for Uncle Charles, our relatives treated us like outcasts. This was a very sensitive issue with my parents.

It was an exciting reunion with Uncle Charles. The next evening, after Dad got off work, he took his brother out for drinks.

My mother, who was always angry about something, now seemed to have an even bigger chip on her shoulder. I remember how she used to make my sister and me come in early almost every day, long before the other kids in the neighborhood. And we didn't come in early to do homework either. I believe she did it so she would not feel lonely, since my father was hardly ever at home, and when he was, they acted like strangers toward one another.

Shortly after my father and uncle arrived home that night, an argument broke out between my parents. The moment I heard them raise their voices, my heart began to race.

I jumped out of bed, put on my clothes and Converse sneakers, as I had done so many times before. I was 10 years old, still a kid, but tough. In the projects you learned early on how to take care of yourself in more ways than one. I knew I might have to break up another fight.

I knelt on the floor. "Please God, take this anger and temper away from my parents," I prayed. Somehow, Uncle Charles was able to calm them down and prevent a physical fight. But this sort of confrontation happened almost every week in our home and was usually handled by my sister and me.

For some strange reason, my mother was immediately calmed by Uncle Charles. Little did we realize she was still a volcano smoldering inside. She calmly stepped over to the sink, put some water in a pot and placed it on a burner. No one thought anything of the fact that she was boiling water. Suddenly, she took the pot from the stove, turned to my father — who had his back to her — and threw the boiling water on him. Then all hell broke loose.

I have never understood why my mother ran into the bathroom and locked the door when she could have run through the kitchen and out the front door. It was as though she had a death wish because she knew my father was going to "kick her butt."

It didn't take long. With a surge of rage, he kicked open the door. My mother was curled up on the floor under the sink. But before dad could put his hands on her, my Uncle Charles and I grabbed him. I also tried to take a kitchen knife from him, but he had such a strong grip, that when I tried to pull the knife from his hand my finger went across the blade, cutting me severely.

As the blood gushed from my fingers, all the attention was immediately shifted to me. Once again, my mother would survive another "barn burner" by the "skin of her teeth."

A common problem I had as child was trying to channel my anger and fears, but not being able to. Frustration upsets the child who cannot rationalize his feelings, and makes him feel angry and powerless. There is no one to turn to, no source of help. Carrying these emotions around with me day after day made me feel like a volcano ready to explode.

I was scared and I didn't know how to talk to my parents about my insecurities. I didn't know how to solve my problems. They just seemed to grow and magnify other problems.

My father was a good provider, but he didn't spend much time at home. I was angry with him for never being there, but I was afraid to tell him so. Of course, if I had told him, he still wouldn't have changed, so I kept getting angry at the wrong people.

I noticed how I would get angry with my sister, Linda, for the slightest thing. She and I would often end up arguing and fighting with each other but usually, neither of us understood why.

We didn't have a clue that we were imitating our parents. We were both frustrated and this was another way of getting our parents' attention. We had no role models who could show us how to behave in ways that would make us feel good about ourselves.

Our lives were miserable because we all had so many negative emotions stewing inside us. These feelings, so deeply lodged within our subconscious minds, would haunt us for years.

People know the saying, "the grass is always greener on the other side of the fence" means that whatever you haven't got is exactly the thing you want. The thing I didn't have and deeply wanted was love. But being young and full of wonder, I discovered many simple pleasures during those years that helped me keep loving life and myself.

Occasionally, on my way home from school, I would slip away to a nearby pond to catch tadpoles. My sister knew how much I enjoyed this and would always tell on me if she found out — not because she was concerned about my well-being, but to "put me in the dog house" with our parents. But I was willing to risk it, because when I stood on the bank of a creek, something inside me shouted with joy.

Our housing project had nature as a neighbor. Nearby, fields and miles of open land were filled with creeks and ponds. Nature's wealth and abundance was at our fingertips.

My friends and I would shed our sneakers and wade into the water, tad poling. The water would ripple and crickets would begin to chirp. Water bugs raced across the pond. A bullfrog would "huh-rok!" as we waited for our prey to appear. We lowered our jars, ready to scoop the first tadpole that passed. Ah, here comes one, he swims closer...flash! The jar scoops in for the catch. "We've got him!"

The tadpoles we kept we put into a plastic dish filled with water and soggy leaves. As the days went by, I would watch their growth as they eventually turned into frogs.

When I was 10 years old, I could not intellectually explain what life was offering me, but I believe I sensed the natural rhythm with nature's simple pleasures of life that gave me confidence to carry on another day.

Looking back on my childhood, I believe that curiosity and love of nature *and sports* kept alive in me an excitement for life, for wanting to know more, to do more. I think I learned to calculate the mysteries of life by plunging into the muddy ponds and creeks.

"Twelve Steps and Twelve Traditions," one of the handbooks for Alcoholics Anonymous, says, "When a drunk has a terrific hangover because he drank heavily yesterday, he cannot live well today. But there is another kind of hangover which we all experience whether we are drinking or not. That is the emotional hangover, the direct result of yesterday's and sometimes today's excesses of negative emotion. If we wish to live serenely today and tomorrow, we need to eliminate these hangovers."

Because my parents fought, they were always harboring resentment and didn't communicate *effectively* with their children. We always felt that we had to "walk on egg shells" and never felt free to express and share our feelings. There seemed to be no cure for our emotional hangovers.

Yet, during the 12 years my family and I lived in the project, I was totally unaware of how my frequent visits to the ponds flooded my senses and reached down to the darkest corners of my mind, giving me hope. When I watched the transformation of a tadpole to a frog, I felt a spiritual connection that life was always evolving to a higher form.

I always dreamed of the day that I would be grown and could leave home and not have to put up with my parents' oppression. I had no idea then how these early family experiences shaped my belief and values, so that even when I left home, the insecurities and bitterness followed me into adult life.

When I finally moved out of the house I had to find out who I was. The hardest part of facing my insecurities was discovering what it was that made me afraid.

The late Virginia Satir, a leading expert on families, said that 98 percent of American families are dysfunctional. My parents were violently dysfunctional. There is a common denominator among alcoholics, foodaholics, gamblers, workaholics, sexaholics, and neurotic parents: each is controlled by a negative habit. These habits cause people to lose touch with their feelings because they have tried to make them disappear through addictions. They also suggest that there are a lot more addicts than we realize. But we limit this area by focusing mostly on drug abuse or alcohol.

A solution depends on two things. The most important one is sporting the right attitude; the other is having the ability to face what drives us to drink, gamble, fight or overeat — submit to those addictions that hide us from our real feelings.

The family is the basic unit of society. It answers the human need to be nurtured, to belong, to feel secure in the love of others, to be a part of something that matters.

When one parent is dysfunctional, according to John Bradshaw in his book "The Family," the whole family system is upset and reacts accordingly. Therefore, the entire family must be treated as a single patient in order to get to the core of individual problems.

The price we pay for not saying how we feel can be dear indeed. It's very important to verbalize our feelings and try to realize the hurt and the need for love behind our behavior. It's important to communicate and share our feelings to keep our anger and frustration from exploding inside us.

If we go through life holding in hurt, we lose our perspective as human beings. In time, our confusion will definitely take its toll psychologically and emotionally.

We can think of the family as a sports team. When we think of sports, we probably think of a team concept: one group of athletes competing against another. Each team works toward a common goal: to win its league championship and become the best team in the state or nation. And when the team wins or loses a game, it affects each player psychologically and emotionally.

In team sports like basketball, football, soccer, hockey and baseball, each player plays a certain position or role, an individual link that allows the team structure to exist. The guiding principle of team concept is wholeness: the whole is greater than the sum of its parts. Only to the extent that the team members operate and function together as a whole unit will the results on the field be successful.

The key to each individual player's success depends largely on the attitude between player and coach — an attitude which can be built up or torn down by the coach and his assistant.

The team concept in sports is a lot like the family-as-a-system, forming a unified whole.

By looking at the family as a system we can see that parents emotionally support their children in much the same way a coach supports the team players to develop and maintain a healthy outlook.

Unless the coach — or parent(s) — works collectively and individually with the "team's players," then the techniques alone won't be enough. "Recipes in books don't bake cookies, people do." "Blueprints on paper don't build bridges, people on a team do." A parent's lectures aren't enough. She or he must interact with a child through loving and caring.

The most important relations we will have are those with our families. We need a parent/coach to help us develop the mental and physical skills to handle life's ups and downs. If they are not present in our lives, it's helpful to find someone else. Perhaps a mentor, a teacher, or someone in the church to help guide us. We have to ask for help sometimes, and be open to answers.

Children who are emotionally abandoned, rejected, hurt or shamed will adjust to stress by creating certain roles to help them survive. We create images to protect ourselves. Some people pretend to be tough and others act as if nothing can bother them — both hiding their pain.

We grow from a child's body to an adult body. But even when we've developed to the point where we look and talk like adults, deep within, there remains a child who never got his needs met.

When we are children and our needs are not met, we could become dysfunctional. We search for love in all the wrong places and for all the wrong reasons. Children often make compromises to try to satisfy the need for acceptance and approval. But, by being compromised, we cannot find direction. If we block out our real needs and feelings, that energy does not die. It surfaces in self-destructive ways.

As adults we may find ourselves continuing to play the same roles we played as children to protect ourselves in our dysfunctional families.

I found myself playing several of the many kinds of roles: the Hero, the Perfect Child, the Scapegoat, and the Rebel.

The Hero brings dignity to the family system. The rationale is, "If I'm good enough and smart enough my family members won't fight. I'll be so good that they will get along." Through my sportsmanship, awards, newspaper articles and scholarship offers, I brought pride back into our family. This was my child's way of creating a family I could be proud of: taking control of what I could.

The Perfect Child is the one who always tries to do things to please his parents. So many times I did things merely to please them. I was seldom concerned about my own happiness.

The Scapegoat is the child who acts out all the anger and pain. He will be the one the family blames for its problems. The attention is taken off the real problems of the family and placed on this child. I used to pick fights with my sister, in acting out my anger and pain. My family would blame me for their problems. They wondered why I couldn't behave.

The Rebel is the family member who tends to break away from the family. He or she is different and often stands alone in their perspective on the home environment. I was so angry at the violence going on in my family that I was determined to get out of the house and have a life of my own at any cost. I didn't want to repeat the same kind of lifestyle that my parents were demonstrating. I tried to stay out of the house as much as possible.

In John Bradshaw's book "The Family," he writes: "The major factor in getting out of a dysfunctional family is awareness about abuse and dysfunctionality." But usually, the more we try to change, the more we stay the same, because we have no new thoughts or information to break the old beliefs that continue to bind the family system and keep us trapped.

We don't have to wait for a catastrophe in order to bring our families closer together. There is so much information and help available today that all we need to do is open ourselves up and be willing to see the truth. We should let ourselves off the hook for a lot of our family history simply isn't our fault. When we can do this, we may be able to find inner peace and help our families by being the light.

Very few people have the perfect families. Even those families who appear to have wonderful relationships, have problems behind closed doors. Our families' difficulties can help us to build our character, and become stronger. Conflicts with our parents are a way of teaching us to become a better person. If you are without parents, their absence teaches you to become stronger and self-reliant. If we can't find the love from our families, we can still love ourselves. In this book, you will find ways to build your self-confidence, love yourself, and to sport the right attitude.

## RECAPS

1) Look at your anger and resentment. These are normal feelings. Are there problems in your family? Have you been removed from your family? Did someone die, or leave? Do you feel angry that they left?
2) Stop blaming. When a situation arises that triggers those insecure emotions, ask yourself, "Why do I feel this way?" Just being aware helps us to heal.
3) Communicate your feelings. Find a friend, counselor, teacher, or someone to confide in. If you can't, sit down and write your thoughts in a journal. If words don't come easily, draw what you feel. Don't edit your words or drawing, just go with what you feel. Get into a habit of putting your feelings on paper. Oftentimes keeping things bottled up is what causes us to do things and say things that get us into trouble. If you

think this may hurt someone, keep the drawing or writings to yourself.

4) Are there other positive ways you can channel your feelings? (music, sports, art, helping others?)
5) Know if your feelings are overwhelming, especially depressive feelings, and you feel like you want to hurt yourself or others, this is a time to seek help. Talk to someone you know can help you. If you can't find someone, call information operator for a hotline to help you.
6) Sporting the Right Attitude is thinking like a star athlete. Know that if you feel you are losing, or that you have lost... you can still win. Don't give up.

## AFFIRMATIONS

Affirmations help us to change our thinking from negative to positive. They work when we memorize them and actually start to feel and visualize what we affirm. "I am" is used to affirm that we already are, what we wish to become. Read the affirmation chapter of this book to learn how to write powerful affirmations that will help you. Here are a few:

I am using these experiences in my family to become a better person.

I am a stronger person because of these family challenges.

(If your parents are absent in your life physically or emotionally)

I am loving myself more despite my parents not being here for me.

## CHAPTER 2

# "I Miss the Home Boys"

*"Death is not the greatest loss in life.*
*The greatest loss is what dies inside us while we live."*

NORMAN COUSINS

I REMEMBER WHEN we moved from the projects to our own single-family residence. My father used his G.I. Bill to buy a beautiful three-bedroom house with a nice large back yard in a quiet community. This was a big mental adjustment for me. I missed my "home boys" in the project, and as often as possible I returned to visit, but my after-school involvement with sports made it difficult.

Despite our having moved to better surroundings, my parents continued to fight and argue. Nevertheless, I got more seriously involved in pursuing my dream of becoming a professional athlete. I put all my time into developing my talents to the fullest, going from one sport to the next, from the football field to the basketball court, to the track and baseball field, year after year.

In the summer of my junior year at Edison High School, a family from Oakland, California, moved into the neighborhood. They purchased a home located diagonally across from our home. Their son, Ellis Porter, stood every bit of 6'5" and was an incredibly talented basketball player. Eventually, we met and became the best of friends.

Ellis would invite me over to play some one-on-one basketball. Sometimes we just talked. Playing against him improved my basketball game greatly. In fact, with his addition to our varsity basketball team, we had one of the tallest starting lineups for a high school basketball team in California that year. We went on to win our league championship and were invited to compete in the Camellia City Tournament of Champions in Sacramento.

In addition to Ellis' basketball talent, I respected and admired his family. His father was a well-read, intelligent man who could discuss any subject. His mother was always very hospitable to me.

There were times I would go over to their house. Mr. Porter would be sitting in his rocking chair, smoking a pipe and reading a book. Ellis' mother might be doing chores or cooking for the family. Sometimes I would go over to their house just to talk with Ellis' father. He would stimulate my mind in many areas beside sports. They never knew about the violence between my parents and I did not volunteer the information. Unconsciously, Mr. Porter may have been the father figure I never had and always wanted.

Mr. Porter often told us, "You will have many mountains to climb and you will be faced with many challenges. But, just carry on, and one day something will happen. Then, you'll realize that your good wouldn't have happened if not for your previous challenges." He always spoke with a deep sense of inner peace and conviction. His conversations about life made me think deeply about the thoughts that stood in the way of my making good choices.

It's important, if we do not have positive role models in our family, to reach out and find them — a neighbor, coach, friend, teacher, employer, or someone to talk to. It's important to vent your feelings.

In his book, "The Language of Feelings," David Viscott writes: "Not to be aware of one's feelings is worse than being blind, deaf and paralyzed. Because those defenses that have blocked our unpleasant memories are also blocking the pleasurable ones."

Many of us have lost — or perhaps have never developed — those positive feelings about ourselves to overcome obstacles. Finding others to talk to can help us to stop replaying in our minds those tragedies that trigger our pain and continue to block our happiness. Those "old tapes" are the primary reasons we stay trapped.

Some of us think that those negative feelings somehow vanish into air over time and our lives become more manageable as we grow older. Some people feel we are just like our parents and we should not expect to be happy or have a positive outlook.

In dysfunctional families, most of what we really need to know about how to live and handle our internal feelings is not taught to us by our parents. They may be too busy trying to make their own lives work.

This is a very important concept. It is human to want acceptance. We feel secure because we have been given our parents' love and approval from day one. We learn that our family loves us. Because they do, the opinion of others doesn't matter. But what happens to the child who is abused, neglected, or whose parents don't know how to love, or are not there? Who do not know how to affirm him or her?

If we are lucky, we learn from our teachers how to better ourselves intellectually. But even so, we're torn down mentally by schoolmates if we don't excel academically or socially, or if we don't wear designer clothes.

Advertisers tell us that wearing the "right" clothes or driving the "right" car will put us out in front of the race: "He who would win must look like a winner." We are constantly fed these unrealistic messages about success. As a result, we often adopt false standards.

Intellectual and social achievements play major roles in showing us how to either suppress or express our feelings and validate our self-worth. Regardless of what we can learn from these experiences at school, we must accept more responsibility for cleaning up our lives. All of us have to find our own path and work out our own destiny. We can change what we don't like about ourselves.

Change can only come when we want to change. In other words, we have to have a good attitude and have faith that we can become better.

Dennis Conner wrote a story for *Sports Illustrated* magazine about how he won the America's Cup. "The Cup represents the ultimate test in the game of life," the yachtsman said. "Just as in life, success demands commitment and commitment demands a positive winning attitude. I told all the guys who came into our Cup campaign that if they were going to make the grade they needed three essential ingredients: attitude, attitude and attitude."

ESPN Sports Announcer, Kellen Winslow, was a tight end for the San Diego Chargers, when the team was named pro football team of the quarter century, 1960-1984. When the team was chosen, he was the only active offensive player honored.

Winslow learned to get in touch with his feelings despite playing such a macho sport. "My first five years in the NFL I didn't have the inner peace I needed off the field," he said. "I don't care how much money you have, if you don't have peace of mind and feel content with yourself, you've got a problem. I cry in church and I don't mind if people see my tears. If one of my boys cries about something, I don't tell him he's a sissy. I comfort him and help him develop the right attitude, because I think it takes a real man to show his feelings."

Males are often considered sissies if they don't play sports or otherwise live up to a macho image. Most men are really afraid to let go of the macho image of themselves. They fear others will find out that they are not as tough and strong as they pretend to be.

Men are not born with a macho image of themselves, no more than we are born with any of our belief systems. Attitudes are learned from others. I don't care how strong, how big or how bad we think we are, as humans we all have certain attitudes and problems that we have to deal with.

Dexter Manley, 6'3"and 257 pounds, led the Washington Redskins to two Super Bowls. Not surprisingly, he found himself forced to fit into the macho image.

In a *Sports Illustrated* article Rick Reilly writes: "There were times when I think Dexter wanted to back down but couldn't" says his college buddy

L.P. Williams. "He had to live up to the image people had of him. This meant talking big and playing big to cover his loneliness."

Most of Manley's life he had an attitude of having to prove himself. As a youth he was trying to constantly win his father's approval because his brother seemed to be the favorite son. He might have succeeded, if he hadn't gotten his girlfriend pregnant during his senior year in high school. "Marry her," said the girl's mother. "Don't you dare," said his father. Manley said he would marry his girlfriend to please her mother, but he would not tell his father. When Manley's father found out, he was furious.

Manley never had the opportunity to explain. When he departed for his first summer at Oklahoma State, he was unaware that his father was dying from colon cancer.

On June 15, Manley's father died. His grief was terrible. He was consumed with the guilt of feeling he had betrayed his father.

After his father's death, says Manley, the family started deteriorating. They even fought over their father's belongings. Before long, Manley's older brother, Reggie, started drinking heavily and smoking marijuana.

Just before Manley returned to college he pleaded with Reggie: "Be very careful, I'm worried something is going to happen to you. Just be careful." It was as though he sensed something awful would happen.

Not long after that, Reggie was robbed and murdered. Luckily, Manley still had football, but because of his performance during practice and games, the coach told him he was never going to amount to anything but a factory worker or a ditch digger. Manley thanked him for that day, because it was the challenge he needed to try harder.

He was driven to become the best.

Now his mother was in bad shape. She had a brain tumor. She was also a diabetic and had undergone a mastectomy. She had to learn how to walk, talk and eat again. Manley now had to help support his mother and his sister who was their mother's caretaker.

All the responsibility thrown on him may have been instrumental in his problems with drugs and alcohol. He eventually checked himself into a rehabilitation center.

No one can change our past or our early family experiences, but we can forgive and release them. One way we can release those hurts and pains that people have caused us to feel, is to talk to them lovingly about our feelings. Use the "I feel" words. "I feel (this way ____ ) when you, ________." If you simply cannot communicate with them, write a letter. But don't give it to them if you think it could hurt them. Even if that person is dead, you can write a letter. Sometimes just writing to a person without mailing the letter helps to relieve the anger and hurt. It is a way to get it off our chests without being judged for how we feel.

Manley wrote a letter to his father after his father died. "I told him I was mad at him, that he never told me he loved me," he said. That letter helped Manley deal with the emptiness he had experienced for so long. We can't always control how others treat us, but we can choose how we react to their attitudes and have the courage to heal ourselves.

Dorothy Briggs recommends in her book, "Celebrate Your Life," to become parents to ourselves. We can try to become the type of parents we wish we had. Think back to what would have brought you joy as a child and re-create it for yourself.

If we make a conscious decision to do something about our early negative programming and stay with it, we will experience changes in all parts of our lives. Our lives can begin to flow without strain or frustration because we are learning to trust our true selves.

The true self within each of us gives us the feeling that we are in touch with something real and it does something to us from within. It is a mysterious something that is easy to recognize but difficult to define.

In "Creative Visualization," Shakti Gawain says, "We have all had experiences of being connected with our true self or higher selves although we may not have conceptualized it in that way. Feeling exceptionally high, clear, strong, on top of the world, or able to move mountains, are indications of being connected to your higher self."

In order to receive inspiration from within, we must first be intensely interested in solving our particular problem or challenge. Only then will creative ideas become unblocked and allowed to flow freely.

In my adult life I continued to blame my parents for all my failures. I was angry and felt they should have known better. After all, they were adults, I told myself.

Later, I discovered that forgiving helps us to get on the right path and get in touch with our higher selves. We must remember, if our parents had known better, they would have done better. So, until we learn to forgive, we cannot release our past. When we are free from resentment, we will succeed in conquering challenges that once seemed impossible to overcome.

Achieving success begins by being willing to change the image we have of ourselves. If we are willing to lay aside those false self-images and confront our emotions realistically, it is possible to overcome negative feelings of weakness, strain and fatigue. Using the tools of faith and forgiveness we can relieve our pain and uncertainty. With faith, knowing things will get better, and a forgiving attitude, we are training our mind and body to operate at peak performance just like athletes who train for the big competitions.

## RECAPS:

1) Accept your feelings.
2) Beware of trying to find inner peace through substance abuse, drugs and alcohol. The long-term effects are severely damaging.
3) Forgive to free yourself of the past and others.
4) Write a letter to express your feelings if you cannot speak to someone face-to-face.
5) Use the "I feel" words. Example: "I feel hurt when you ___ ___."

6) Beware of advertiser's messages. Often they are hidden messages to make you feel you aren't good enough if you don't have (whatever they are selling.) ______."
7) It's ok to cry.

## AFFIRMATIONS:

Today, I am becoming a better person.

Today, I release the ideas that money, power and approval from others determine my success.

Today, I determine my own success.

Today, I know that I am being guided toward my real purpose in life.

## SPORT THE RIGHT ATTITUDE!

CHAPTER 3

# Why Me?

*"The mind is its own place, and in itself can*
*Make heaven of hell, a hell of Heaven."*

John Milton

My senior year in high school I experienced a drastic event that turned my life inside out. It made my days seem like weeks and my weeks seem like months.

On a Friday night in Stockton, after a football game, a friend came by my house to see me. He wanted me to go with him on a joy-ride to Modesto, which was 28 miles away. My first instinct was to say "no," but I decided to go anyway. We left and picked up a few other friends along the way.

We were a happy carload of teen-agers ready to party. But about 18 miles out of Stockton, on Highway 99, we were forced off the road by a drunken driver. Lemore, my best friend and the front seat passenger, was thrown out the front window as the car turned over and slid 290 feet. Leroy and I (two of the three back-seat passengers) were thrown out of the rear side windows. The driver and the other passenger somehow remained in the car. Paramedics found Leroy and me underneath a chain-link fence 120 feet from where the car stopped.

An ambulance unit rushed us to San Joaquin General Hospital in Stockton. I was unconscious when we arrived. Lemore died in en route to the hospital.

We were placed in separate rooms until doctors arrived and families came to identify us. Somehow Lemore and I had been misidentified as each other.

When my parents arrived, they were told their son, "Walter," was dead. When they went into the room to identify the body, they were relieved to find out that it was not me.

When I was eventually located, my father burst into tears. The nurse told my parents my condition appeared quite serious, which it was. I was in a coma having sustained a skull fracture, a broken shoulder and multiple internal injuries.

Doctors told my parents that I needed an operation to correct an injured scalp bone which would take several hours, and suggested they go home and come back later. My father refused to go, but my mother went home to gather her emotions and rest.

After my operation, my father was told that my condition was critical and my chances for survival were not good.

Here I was, in a fight for my life, the biggest challenge I had ever experienced. It was a battle greater than anything I could have faced running track, or playing on the basketball court, or the football and baseball fields.

When word got out about my condition, carloads of school mates, coaches and teachers filled the hospital corridors. That weekend the hospital had to call in extra security to make sure no one entered the room but my parents.

Two days went by and I remained in critical condition. My father was at the hospital nearly around the clock. The doctor had done the surgery. The rest was up to God and me.

There's an old saying, "The doctor dresses the wound, but God heals it." No physician or surgeon claims that he healed the patient. The one healing power is called by many names — God, Jesus Christ, Buddha, Life, Creative Intelligence, the Universal Mind, Allah...and many others.

To the doctor's amazement, on the third day I came out of the coma. On the fourth day I was still being fed intravenously, but I was taken off the critical list. From somewhere deep within, I had begun to fight for life and was winning. I believe it was that competitive spirit I developed from sports that helped me refuse to give up on life.

In a *Runner's World* magazine article, sports specialist Edward Coyle says that athletes retain some long-term psychological benefits from exercise even after training has ceased.

Doctors know from experience that a patient with a fighting spirit and a positive attitude seems to have a better chance of recovery than one who surrenders to their illness.

Norman Cousins, in his book "Anatomy of An Illness," writes about having been told he had a disease of the spine. He was told he had one chance in 500 of surviving it and would probably never walk again.

Cousins had read Han's Selye's classic book "The Stress and Distress of Life," in which Selye details the effects of negative emotions on body chemistry. He believed that if negative emotions produce negative chemical changes in the body, then positive emotions should produce positive chemical changes.

Cousins decided he was not going to give in to his disease. In hopes of healing himself, he ordered Marx Brothers movies and old "Candid Camera" episodes. What he discovered was laughter and a positive attitude enhanced his body's ability to fight inflammation and set in motion the mechanisms of self-healing.

This incident made him realize the importance of the thoughts we think: the direction they take actually constitutes our will to live or die.

My parents were overjoyed when they learned that my condition had changed for the better. I had spent my life as a teenager developing my athletic skills, hoping that someday I would be on television playing for a professional team. I had set school records, won awards and trophies and received scholarship offers stemming from my Most Valuable Player awards. But immediately after the accident, the scholarship offers vanished and for the first time in my life I lost all confidence in myself.

Now, I was frightened about the future. But I was unable to let go of the past, because I had put all of my energy and even my will to live into sports.

Elvin Hayes, the former National Basketball Association Champion scorer and re-bounder, said, "The worst moment in an athlete's life is discovering that forever isn't very long. The kids playing now think they're going to play forever."

Nine days after I entered the hospital I was released. For weeks, I was like an infant, unable to do anything for myself. One morning I wandered away from the house. Friends found me and brought me back home.

After about one month, I was coherent enough to realize what had happened. When I did, I was filled with anger and resentment. "Why me?" I asked myself over and over. I blamed my mother for not telling me to stay home that fateful night. I blamed my father for never being there when I craved his love and affection. I didn't know whether I should blame the driver and retaliate against him. I blamed everyone but myself.

In calculating my fear against my need to get back on course, one thing was certain: No matter how many people I chose to blame for my condition or how much frustration I was feeling, if I was to rebuild my life, I could not do it if I held on to negative thoughts. Somehow, I would have to keep my thoughts on a higher level and as far from the problem as possible to be able to move past it.

Two months passed before my doctor decided that I was physically and mentally able to return to school. By this time I was afraid I might have lost my athletic talents. I had become the first Edison High School athlete to letter in four different sports (football, basketball, baseball and track and field) in one school year, two years in a row. I was also attempting to accomplish that in my senior year before my accident.

My recovery was one of the most difficult periods in my life. I had to trust myself because I had no one else to turn to. My parents were distressed and I didn't know how to reach out to them. The accident did bring us closer together, but only for a moment. I had to face the lonely and painful days ahead alone.

## RECAPS

1) During the course of our lives we may experience events that turn our lives inside out. It's not life that makes us or breaks us, it's how we accept what has happened to us.
2) The greatest fight in our life will be the battle within ourselves. We have to be aware and stand guard against our negative thoughts that keep us from our good.
3) When maintaining a physical exercise program for a long time, we can maintain the long-term positive psychological benefits even if we stop exercising.
4) Doctors know from experience that a patient with a fighting spirit and a positive attitude seems to have the greatest chance of recovery from illness.
5) "If negative emotions produce negative chemical change in the body, then positive emotions should produce positive chemical changes." — Norman Cousins.
6) One of the greatest crimes is to not strive to better ourselves.
7) Giving up resentment and blaming others for circumstances in our lives will empower us with the energy and mental freedom we need to change for the better.

## AFFIRMATIONS

Today, every challenge will bring me closer to the place I desire to be.

Today, I will look to the future knowing my life is going to be better.

Today, I refuse to allow anything or anyone to condemn me.

Today, I am now being all that I can be.

## SPORT THE RIGHT ATTITUDE!

CHAPTER 4

# You Can't Give Up

*"The difference between the impossible and the possible lies in not giving up."*

Tommy Lasorda,
*Legendary Baseball Hall of Famer*

The football season had ended and my doctor would not release me to play basketball. Despite his restricting all my activities for several months, I was determined to pursue my dream to become a professional athlete.

I started working out long hours alone on the basketball court trying to regain my athletic skills. My stubborn side would not surrender to my setback. Instead, I worked harder than ever to make San Joaquin Delta's Junior College basketball team.

I resented having to go to junior college, but then, as I thought about it, I felt I would have the time to rebuild my confidence by making the junior college team. There was still a chance to get an athletic scholarship to a four-year university if I could prove I hadn't lost my ability.

When I was participating in sports I felt good about myself. I believed I was in total control and there was nothing I could not do. But it was also during this time that I began to consider what I would do without sports in my life. If I didn't make the squad, how much would I miss people cheering for me at games? Most of all, I knew I'd miss the way my friends looked up to me. The good opinion of your peers is very important when you're growing up.

I just could not imagine life without basketball or some kind of organized sports. Sports had played such an important role in my life for so long. It helped fill the void that was left by a family who could not emotionally be there for me. I realized that sports was what made me feel accepted and loved.

These factors became the motivating force that intensely drove me to make a comeback. After a long struggle, I made the team and my life was once again moving forward.

As the weeks and months passed, things seemed to be getting better. Then another tragedy struck. On New Year's Eve my father and some friends were entering a nightclub just as a man was being bounced out for his disruptive behavior. When the man tried to go back in, my father tried to calm him down. Within seconds the man stabbed my father.

When I arrived home about two o'clock that morning, I noticed that a car belonging to Maggie Williams (one of my mother's friends) was parked in front of the house and all of the living room lights were on. When I walked in the door, Maggie told me my father had been stabbed and was at St. Joseph's Hospital, where my mother waited. I borrowed her car and raced through the streets. I can remember I had a hard time seeing the road through my tears.

When I arrived at the hospital, my dad was in surgery. My mother and sister were with a few friends in the waiting area. Everyone was silently waiting for the outcome. When the doctor finally came out, he told us my father's condition was critical, and they were moving him to Intensive Care on the third floor.

In total shock from the doctor's statement, we went to Intensive Care to be by my father's side. There were moments he would open his eyes and even attempt to talk. At one point I was alone with him at his bedside, watching him fight for is life. But he wasn't aware of who I was in his condition.

Standing there, many thoughts crossed my mind. I thought about all the things I wanted to say to him. He was the man I had spent 18 years with and I knew so little about his childhood. We never spent any really meaningful moments together. We didn't share our feelings or stories with one another. I wished he had given me a perspective, a set of principles and values I could use to adapt to the real world. I couldn't recall our family ever sharing outings or holidays together. Instead, we lived in a loveless home environment that hampered our expression as individuals. I realized that I was locked in the dilemma faced by many people who are raised in a violent family. In such a home, you don't learn how to give or receive affection. And when you are hurting inside you refuse to let yourself cry.

Regardless of my father's shortcomings, I still pleaded and begged God not to take his life. I thought maybe this second "near death" experience would make our family appreciate one another and enjoy life as a healthy unit. My accident hadn't changed things, but I wanted to believe my father's stabbing would definitely bring our family closer together.

I left his room and told my mother that I was going to the cafeteria to get something to eat. But as I sat at the lunch counter, I couldn't eat. I feared that my father would die. I decided to go back up stairs to see if his condition had changed. It had. When I stepped out of the elevator, I ran into my mother and sister clutching each other, sobbing. I didn't have to ask. I knew. My father was dead.

I'm not openly emotional by nature, but on that day, I came completely apart. I didn't just weep, I screamed. For days, I cried off and on and I couldn't sleep at night. I never felt so out of control in all my life. Not even after my accident did I experience such mental anguish and loneliness.

My father and I didn't have a good relationship. There was a tremendous amount of unexpressed love screaming from within me. When we suffer the sudden death of a loved one, it makes the process of grieving more difficult. There is disbelief about what has happened and we feel bewildered. The person is gone, but their memory is still present.

"If we don't grieve, we become chronically disoriented," says Glen Davidson, professor of psychiatry at Southern Illinois University School of Medicine. "To fully recover and move forward past the immediate loss, we must affirm and acknowledge our feelings."

According to Dr. Davidson, author of "Living With Dying and Understanding Mourning," feelings of sorrow, guilt, anger, depression, loneliness, fear, anxiety and shame are all normal emotions associated with bereavement that need to be voiced openly and honestly. Dr. Davidson also says, "Only through telling our story over and over again do we clarify in our own minds what has happened and how we really feel about it. Through that we come to accept the reality of the loss so we can go on living."

Some losses seem unfair, but part of life is learning how to adjust to loss and coming to terms with the perceived unfairness.

I was terrified to say good-bye to a part of my history that meant so much. There was so much I wanted to know. I knew so little about my father's history. There are no words powerful enough to express the pain and loss of a family member or anyone you love deeply.

Confused and disillusioned, I dropped out of school for months. I wandered the streets, not really knowing where to go or what I could do. The inner turmoil of not being sure of myself or my objective in life was compounded by my father's sudden death. However, the weaker I became, the more courage and strength my mother seemed to display. I had never seen such power in her before. I couldn't understand how she could be so strong when I was filled with such helplessness. Even today her words still ring loudly in my ears: "Somehow we will make it, son. I just want to see you finish college. You need to get a solid education, something you can use for the rest of your life. You can't dribble a basketball the rest of your life. Make something of yourself. Don't be a quitter."

My mother's greatest dream was to see her children acquire a good education because she had not gotten very far in school. I asked myself. "What else can I do? I don't want to be a junkie, user, or a drug dealer. I don't want to poison the world." The idea of pursuing a college degree did not sink in immediately, but I began to think about the idea more often. It was apparent I was not going to receive a sports scholarship, so I had to come to grips with the fact that I needed to get a college degree.

Looking back on my athletic career, there was one coach who stood out in my mind: my high school assistant football coach, Ben Parks. When Parks said "Jump!" we asked "How high?"

Without a doubt, out of all the coaches I played for, he was the most inspirational man in my life. He believed that regardless of what your talents were, if you're willing to give 100% everyday, you could play football for him. He was known as a hard, tough coach who inspired you to believe in yourself.

If you played on the team, you not only wanted to win football games, you developed courage, strength and a positive self-image along the way. Needless to say, this had increased my confidence and enthusiasm in all parts of my life.

One of the most important lessons athletes learn is how to motivate themselves. Even a physically weak athlete becomes stronger by training with the right attitude. Through practice, athletes learn that real growth is achieved when they no longer let their weaknesses get the best of them. Instead, they learn to turn weaknesses into strengths.

I felt that if I could apply the same energy and positive attitudes I used in sports toward academics, maybe I could earn a college degree. I had to believe in the unseen. I had to believe that I was winning the school game, just like I felt when I was running track, playing sports.

If you can believe that you are just as intelligent as your peers, you can succeed in anything you want to accomplish. In addition to having faith, it's just as important to keep believing, no matter what the situation may appear to be. Some of the most exciting games in history were won when a team was getting "slaughtered" or considered underdogs. But, because they didn't give up, that "losing" team came back, overcame the odds, and won.

This is especially true for individuals on a team, who go through obstacles and must find the courage and confidence to make it through those hard periods when others have given up on them.

Tony Dungy, head coach of the 2007 Super Bowl-winning Indianapolis Colts, attributes his faith and belief to him becoming the first African-American football coach to win the championship, and getting him through devastating times.

In 2002 Dungy was fired from his coaching position for the Tampa Bay Buccaneers. However, he didn't give up and quit football. His faith and belief in himself resulted in the Colts hiring him. He went on to lead them to victory. Sadly, this came a little more than a year after his 18-year-old son James, committed suicide. He talks about how faith got him through the obstacles in his memoir, "Quiet Strength: The Principles, Practices, and Priorities of a Winning Life."

Most people would have given up. When a loved one dies, it's especially hard to get through the pain and suffering. Dungy, a spiritual man, feels to get through that kind of tragedy, and any obstacles, you have to have faith.

"There is a confidence that someone bigger is in charge," says Dungy. "God is in charge. And, other people have dealt with this and made it through. Not to give in, not to think my situation is so bad that I can't get through it."

There is a saying that I love: "Don't leave five minutes before the miracle." Dungy did not quit even after he was fired, although he thought of leaving football to become a prison minister. But, he kept believing and he found the inner strength to go on which resulted in his historic victory winning the Super Bowl.

Regardless of how far behind I was in school from physical and emotional problems, I had to keep believing like Dungy, and visualizing my academic skills improving. I had to believe that it was possible to receive a degree from a four-year college.

Sometimes when the going gets rough, and we try to focus on a dream, those we love may tell us the dream cannot happen. Members of our family may be the number-one offenders, not because they are mean, but because they do not believe in themselves. And if they don't believe in themselves, it's hard for them to believe that others can reach their goals. We cannot let ourselves get hurt or discouraged if we are not supported, but simply recognize that our parents may be suffering from low self-esteem.

As children, to survive, we physically and psychologically need our parents, guardians or whomever raises us. We depend on their support for an extended period of time. Our relationship with our family is a key link to society.

Within the family system we are programmed and develop our beliefs about ourselves from the information exchanged. The tape starts rolling, recording our family patterns, and constantly shaping our lives and personalities.

Our emotions are an integration of experiences, beliefs and ideas which eventually become our reality. If, as children, we have not been permitted to experience or express our emotions, they become locked inside us. The repression of our emotions begins in childhood out of an effort to be accepted by our parents and to protect our self worth.

We place more value on what our parents or guardians think of us than on what we think of ourselves, and our sense of self goes down a few notches. When we look at the internal picture of ourselves, there is an enormous amount of confusion going on. Unfortunately, we develop a habit of saying to ourselves, "I'm no good," "I'm not loved," or "I'm a problem child."

Even if we accomplish something that we are proud of, we're afraid to share feelings for fear of being hurt and rejected. We end up blocking our happiness. As the mind is continually obstructed and hampered by these inhibitions, the true and spontaneous self is not permitted to move freely.

When we are children, we see our parents as all-powerful, almost like Gods. Automatically, we accept their values, feeling and moods. The key to a more joyful life, however, lies squarely in a new awareness about how our family experiences shape our inner selves, and how sometimes they block our personal growth. Our parents don't mean to suppress us, but sometimes the way we are brought up can be very damaging to our self-esteem. Our parents may be simply mimicking their parents, who were also misinformed. Remember, if they knew better, they could be better.

Parents do and say things to protect their children. But sometimes, they simply make mistakes. We all do. You do, I do, and the world does.

When you doubt or disagree with your parents, it's important to be honest and ask yourself if you think your parents are trying their best to help or protect you, even if you don't agree. Do you think you simply don't understand one another? Sometimes we blame our parents because we don't see that they made decisions in our lives based on the fears they have in the world and it's for our own good and protection. You may not understand until you become a parent.

Do you feel they simply don't care, and are preoccupied with other people or things? Perhaps they have addictions including alcohol, drugs, work, and other things that keep them from being the parent or guardian you desire. If you feel they have problems beyond a lack of understanding you, it's important to look back and examine the ways our parents or guardians handled everyday problems. Through this search we can start to understand ourselves. If we're afraid to swim in the ocean, perhaps our parents passed down their fears to us. If we don't think we can succeed in life, maybe our parents felt that way, too. Although we cannot attribute all of our personality quirks to our parents, being able to understand familiar patterns can help us make the changes we want to make in our lives. We can break away from the past, but it sometimes takes some courage.

We can start to unravel the mysteries of why success eludes us in certain areas of our lives by talking to our parents about their childhoods. We can also get answers by questioning the environment in which we grew up. What did the culture have to say to us about who we are and how we should behave? What choices did we have? Were there forbidden things that you could not discuss outside of the house? What was your father's attitude toward you? How did it differ from your mother's? What messages did you get from your guardian? How did they express disapproval? Were they stern? Were their attitudes different for your brother or sister? If so, how did they differ? How did you handle your fear? Did you discuss your fears with your parents or guardians? If not, why? How often did your parents/guardians give you positive feedback about your accomplishments? Do you still seek their praise and acceptance? How often did you feel lonely and angry? Do you feel guilty even asking these questions? If so, why?

Your answers to those questions will help you learn the attitudes of your parents. Parents' attitudes help to create our belief systems. Let me explain what I mean by this. If our parents/guardians constantly tell us we will never be anything or we are good for nothing, in time we begin to believe them, and even act accordingly. This attitude will begin to carry over into other areas of our life.

Some of us do not want to admit that our parent's/guardian's behavior patterns are linked to our own. It is common for children to want to be as much unlike their parents as possible, especially if the parents are not the best role models. However, if we grow up in a positive family climate, our parents build up our self-esteem. It is rare, but possible, to find the "perfect parents," free of hang-ups. Everyone has faults.

Sometimes those negative emotions in our families are so strong; people may feel there is nothing they can do about them, because they're simply in the genes. But that's not true. We have no choice over who our parents are, or living situations as children, but we do have some choices about how we will shape our future.

When we convince ourselves that we are born to fail or that we did not come from the "right" side of the tracks, we're setting ourselves up for a lifetime of insecurity and failure. We are hiding behind those patterns so we don't have to deal with the truth. The truth is that we have to take the responsibility for making our lives better.

What we learn, when we develop the courage to look at our childhood, is that our parents have passed ways of behaving down to us.

Long after we grow up, those passed down values continue to run our lives. And if we don't like those values or beliefs, we can change them. It is all learned, isn't it? If poor behavior is learned, then so is good behavior. If evil and hatred can be learned, so can compassion and appreciation for the positive.

My mother was a victim of my father's bizarre violent behavior for almost 18 years. She may have wondered what she could do to change things for the sake of the children. But consciously or unconsciously, she chose to remain in the relationship, despite how bad it was. Children must simply adjust. As a family, we lived in discomfort because it was familiar. It's change that's scary, even if it is for the better.

Having lived through this confusion and family imbalance for 18 years, I found it difficult to seek advice from either parent as I was recovering from my accident. Because of the family violence and the fact that I was very shy, I isolated myself as often as possible.

But we don't have to live out our lives with those old character defects. Once we admit that we need to improve as people, we can begin to look at the part of ourselves that we don't like as simply a belief about ourselves. The great thing about beliefs is that they can be changed. When we start looking at our assets and what type of people we want to become, we can become free and successful.

## RECAPS:

1) Everyone has problems with their parents or guardians. You are not alone.
2) Whatever our parents taught us during our early years helped shape our belief system and personality.

3) We should seek to understand our family's blueprints and how our parents/guardians handled everyday problems. Through this search we can see that we were handed down their "psychological genes" which can be replaced by higher thoughts about ourselves.
4) When we convince ourselves that we are born to fail, or that we really did not come from the "right" side of the tracks, we're copping out.
5) Change is not easy, especially if we have learned to live with a certain negative behavior pattern. But with right attitudes, we can overcome any obstacles and turn weaknesses into strengths.
6) We have to learn to forgive our parents/guardians. If they knew better, they would have done better. Forgiveness helps to free ourselves so we can go on to live our dreams.

## AFFIRMATION

Today, I can overcome my problems, despite my childhood.
Today, I am changing and becoming a better person.
Today, I have the power within me to overcome the challenges before me.
Everyday in everyway, I'm getting better and better. — Émile Coué

## SPORT THE RIGHT ATTITUDE!

## CHAPTER 5

# Just a Thought Away

*"Perhaps the most valuable result of all education is the ability to make yourself do the thing you have to do, when it ought to be done, whether you like it or not."*

THOMAS HENRY HUXLEY

THE SEMESTER AFTER my father's death I re-registered at junior college. Soon after, I was accepted at Sacramento State University and once again my life began moving forward. At first, I feared going away to college, but I knew I could not let my fear control me.

Robin James, a prolific illustrator of over 30 children books says, "Fear isn't necessarily negative. There's a positive way of being afraid---and that is to be so afraid of missing your good (blessings) that nothing holds you back from trying to get ahead."

My mother tried to offer some advice, but she didn't know enough about higher education to be helpful. Now I would be competing with students who were confident in the academic world that intimidated me. After all, I had spent most of my free time on the basketball courts, not in libraries.

My biggest challenge would be to manage my fear. I knew that to have a chance of making it, I would have to put the same dedication into my studies as I did into playing basketball. But I didn't know what to expect at a four-year college. Before I decided upon a major, I worked to finish general education classes.

Although I was not involved in organized sports, I set up a regular jogging program for myself. These workouts helped me develop the personal program of self-discipline I would need to handle a four-year college.

Ask any runner why he runs and I am sure he won't rave about the workouts. He does it for the feeling, that natural "high." If we're feeling down, jogging, aerobics or any fitness program can bring us up and help our spirits soar.

Scientists and doctors agree that many of the problems people experience as they age are not caused by disease but by lack of exercise. Running is a wonderful way to keep in good physical shape as it reduces stress, keeps our minds sharp; and maintains a healthy heart by keeping it pumping steadily and efficiently for years. Although a certain amount of muscle loss is inevitable as we age, running keeps muscles as firm, fast, and strong as possible. We also can breathe easier. People who are not active lose flexibility in their rib cages as they age, but by running, our muscles all over our body can become stronger.

I had never before been involved in long distance running, but I became totally consumed by it. It became a powerful defense against my problems, as a kind of therapy. Running made me feel totally comfortable in my body, mind, and spirit.

When school let out for the summer, I loaded and unloaded ships' cargo at the Port of Stockton. It was hard work, but a lot easier than the times I used to work in the hot, humid fields picking vegetables and fruits. That was back-breaking work. Even though I was able to handle the demanding physical labor because of my athletic training, I knew I didn't want to do this type of work my entire life. Instead, it gave me a strong incentive to graduate from college. Any menial labor job that we have to take can make us be more determined to be better in life. So instead of complaining, I had to use these types of jobs to motivate me to get my college degree to obtain a better paying job.

At the start of my second semester, I chose social work as a major. I felt a burning desire to help youths raised in depressed neighborhoods like mine. I wanted to help them put their energies into academics and not all into sports, as I had done.

In the Edison Villa projects in Stockton, I had my first encounter with a true superstar athlete. He helped me realize that sports can open doors, but that a college degree can carry you the distance.

Dick Bass was the great running back for the University of the Pacific and the Los Angeles Rams. He had set many football records at UOP. He would occasionally come to the gym in the projects and talk with the kids. Whenever he arrived, word would spread throughout the community and everyone would come running to see him. We wanted to get close enough to touch him, hoping greatness would rub off on us. He was like some kind of deity to us. All of the kids---and many of the adults — worshiped Bass because he gave us hope. He talked to us about believing in ourselves and developing the right attitudes to fight against the odds.

Bass told us that it didn't matter if you did not have the "perfect family," or whether you were raised by one parent, or by relatives. You could still make it if you believed in yourself.

One of my best friends in the projects was Wilbert Miles. He was raised by his mother, a single parent. Wilbert's favorite sport was basketball, and even though he didn't have natural athletic talent, he was a hard worker. Through sheer determination he became a better-than-average player. As a high school senior, he earned respect throughout the league as one of the best forwards in Northern California.

Wilbert was also driven by his mother to work hard academically. She knew it would be easy for him to slip into bad peer groups and become a delinquent. She helped him to set goals and prepare himself at an early age to act without assistance. From his mother's guidance and mental support, Wilbert understood that if he was going to improve his social and economic lifestyle as an adult, an education would make the difference. During Wilbert's three years at Edison High School, he maintained a 3.0 grade point average. His academic scores and basketball performance earned him a four-year athletic scholarship to the University of Santa Clara, where he later graduated.

According to statistics, Wilbert was destined for failure because he was an African-American living in a low-income home and raised by one parent. But we cannot be sucked into what statistics tell us, just as we can't let other people's opinions about us mold our thinking and lead us to believe we can't make it in life.

Granted, there are many people who don't make it coming from those circumstances. But measuring ourselves by society's expectations of us will make us failures every time. We should only compare ourselves with our potential, according to our individual skills and talents. Wilbert didn't look at what others said he should be or should do. He lifted his sights above all obstacles, above the opinions of "experts."

When I returned to school, I spoke with a counselor who helped me figure out what classes I would need to take to graduate with my class. I got so excited about my dream becoming a reality, the following semester I carried 21 units.

The late Pat Summerall, the veteran CBS Sports announcer, had a plaque in his office that read: "Everything cometh to him who waiteth, if they worketh like hell while they waiteth."

At registration for my last semester, when I gave the lady my name, I was told my graduation packet was on hold because I hadn't paid off a loan. My heart fell to my feet. I panicked and did not know what to do.

I didn't know how I would come up with the money. My mother didn't have enough money to help me. There was no one to turn to. What was so painful was that I had overcome a severe accident, struggled to keep up mentally with my peers to pass classes and then, when I was finally on the verge of success, I was being denied a chance to finish school because I had no money. Ironically, I needed to finish school to get money.

My mind raced. What was I going to do? I found myself walking aimlessly around the campus, trying to think of a way to overcome this obstacle. Nothing came to mind. I decided to go back to the registration window and see if I could work out an arrangement to register.

Then a miracle happened.

As I stood in line, I noticed that the woman I had talked to earlier had left. I gave my name to the new person, as if I had just come to register. For some reason, the new person wasn't able to find my packet. I didn't say anything about being there before. I just let her look. The woman who had seen me earlier had taken out my packet and hadn't put it back. By the grace of God, that oversight allowed me to register. Eventually I had to pay back the loan, but by the time my unpaid loan went through the system, I had the money to start repayments.

When some people are told "no" in life, they meekly accept the answer. I've never been that type of person. I love the saying, "Don't give up five minutes before the miracle."

I've always believed there is a way to get what you want if you really believe in the cause and as long as it doesn't hurt anyone in the process. Many times I have found that I had to accept the answer, "no" but seldom do I accept "no" for an answer without challenging the reason why.

Many students take their education and getting a degree for granted. I never did. I wanted to share with everyone how difficult my struggle had been. I can remember my graduation day very clearly. I felt so many emotions as I waited to receive my degree. I wanted to cry. I wanted to dance across the stage.

Even if I had been given the opportunity to speak at graduation, words could not have expressed what I felt as I waited to receive that degree. The dream I had four years earlier, had finally become a reality.

The stadium stands were filled on my graduation day. My eyes searched for my family. It would have made me happy to see my father. I knew he would be proud to see his son receive a college degree.

Those thoughts awakened painful memories. No matter where I looked, he could never be more than a memory. Having learned how sacred life can be, I was humble enough to realize that I was blessed to have memories of him.

Pride is not a matter of feeling superior to other people, but of taking pleasure in one's own achievements. On my graduation day, I found a new strength and confidence that was to change my outlook on life. I had learned that nothing can stop us from getting what we want except ourselves. There may be detours and roadblocks along our path, but remember, they are not permanent unless we make them so.

Refuse to think of failure or to doubt your own power. Refuse to listen to limitations of any kind. "The person who sees what he wants to see regardless of what appears," says Ernest Holmes, Founder of Science of Mind philosophy," will some day experience in the outer what he has faithfully seen within."

## RECAPS

1) Fear isn't entirely negative. There's a positive way of being afraid.
2) Set up regular exercise programs which will become instrumental in giving you self-discipline, release stress, and maintain good health.
3) Decide on what you want to become in life and go for it.
4) You can become successful if you believe in yourself.
5) Disregard statistics, the odds and don't link yourself with those stereotypes.
6) We can always be the exception and not the rule.
7) There may be road blocks along our path, but they're not permanent unless we believe that they are.
8) Refuse to think of failure or to doubt your own power.

## AFFIRMATIONS

Today, I take control of my life with a positive attitude.
Today, I am confident.
Today, I maintain good thoughts about myself.
Today, I have the power to become a success in life.
Today, I am successful.
My good is not limited by who I am or where I come from.

## SPORT THE RIGHT ATTITUDE!

CHAPTER 6

# Overcoming the Silent Enemy... Your Hidden Anger

*Anger is like burning down your house to get rid of the rats.*

HARRY EMERSON FOSDICK

EVERYONE GETS ANGRY. Anger is a normal emotion we all experience at one time or another. Although anger is a typical normal human emotion, it's hardly the most useful for solving problems. But it can be useful if used constructively to rise out of situations that have kept us stuck.

When I saw my father abusing my mother, I used that anger vowing to myself that when I got married, I would never put a hand to my wife, and I have never disrespected my wife that way. Because my father and I didn't have a good relationship, when he was killed I also used that anger I felt about him being emotionally and physically absent. When I had my kids, I always tried to be the best father, and to always be present for them; and I have.

But because I didn't deal with my anger when I was growing up, I suffered with the problem as an adult in other areas of my life. Many adults have anger issues from childhood, that's why I'm writing this chapter so you can be aware, and not carry anger as you mature.

For myself, I found ways as an adult to free myself from the emotion, although it took a long time. I read about and studied anger, its effects on the body, and on other people. I researched it, wrote about it, spoke to groups about anger, and even became a certified anger management consultant trained by George Anderson, the psychologist whose model on anger management was used in the movie "Anger Management," starring Jack Nicholson and Adam Sandler.

But my greatest teacher on the subject of anger was growing up in a low-income housing project with my parents constantly fighting. They both seemed either unconcerned or unaware of the emotional scars this violence would leave on my brother, my sister, and me. Those scars would last me what seems like a lifetime.

Here's what my father taught me about anger. If you are not in touch with your feelings, if you are not in touch with your purpose, and if you are not striving to live your dream by using your talents and gifts to improve and change your circumstances, that anger will keep you stuck. It will control your every action.

See even if we are in a household with arguing parents, we can use our gifts to become better. For me it was my involvement in sports. My wife Janet, who also grew up in a household with a step-father who went on alcoholic rages, wrote about her angry feelings, and became a professional writer for CBS and ABC Television Networks. What can you do? Sing? Write? Work on a hobby? Or maybe there is nothing you can do at the moment with your talents, so write out your goals. If you don't know your talents, read books. Go to a library. You can perhaps discover your gifts and what you would like to do with your talents by reading about other people's experiences.

Some people say, "I don't know what I want to do." "I don't have any talents." Everyone has talents, even if it's only smiling. Do you know that there are people called greeters who smile at customers for a living? They're employed everywhere from Wal*Mart, to Fortune 500 companies, and places like DisneyLand. Maybe that's not what you want to do, but the point is, even something as easy as smiling is a talent that helps light up other people's lives, and lifts their spirits. They set a tone for the company they work for. You have a talent — a gift. What is yours?

It's OK if you don't know what you want to do with your life. Many people at your age don't know. The point is, that you start thinking about your future. Don't worry about money, or how you're going to get there. Just dream. Think of your talents, and then think of what will fit. Some people like to talk a lot, and like to hang out with their friends. If you do too, know that you are a "people person." So what fields could you work with people? Some people work alone like writers and accountants. We all have to interact with people but some jobs require teamwork, like working in an advertising agency, or working as a paramedic. Some doctors work as part of a surgical team. Other doctors, family practitioners, work alone on their treatments. They consult with other doctors occasionally, but the initial work is done alone.

You get the point? If you don't know, research it on a computer at home, at school, or in your local library.

I'll never forget years ago I was the stereotypical angry black man. You know the one they show on the six o'clock news, except I was not breaking the law or standing on the corner selling drugs. I have never been to jail or prison, even though my cousins had, but yes, I was angry. Looking back, I know now I carried anger from the early childhood and teen years.

When you carry that kind of angry energy around on a daily basis, you attract negative situations into your life when you least expect them, even simple occurrences that reflect your hidden anger. I remember I would go to a movie, or a concert, and I would always try to get as close as possible to the stage, which meant my tickets cost a lot of money. Among the thousands of people at the venue, I would always manage to attract the one person in the crowd who would sit directly behind me and kick my seat again and again. I would boil over, and finally have to ask the person to stop kicking my seat. But by that time the event was ruined for me.

Or, I would attract people on the freeway. You know the type on their cell phones yapping away, who would cut me off in traffic. I would brake hard to prevent an accident, and the person cutting me off, would throw me the finger, cursing at me as if it was my fault, then I was sucked into cursing back. This can be dangerous where I live in Los Angeles, because people all the time get shot and killed in road rage.

I remember there were times I would walk into a supermarket and attract the one person who would bump into me without excusing themselves. I would instantly get enraged. See these may be coincidences to some people, but you have to look at negative things repeating themselves in your lives as signs. It's an opportunity to ask, truthfully, "What thoughts am I holding that attract this situation?" Sometimes it's the fear that these things were going to reoccur which bring negative situations. I had to learn to monitor my thoughts when I went to events and not fear that I would attract the seat kicker, because you guessed it, if I did, that person would certainly be behind me kicking my seat.

I once read that anger is a form of fear. When we are so afraid we project anger out to the world. This is why a lot of children feel their parent's anger at them is unjust. But they are afraid their child will get hurt from doing the wrong thing, and instead of explaining to them calmly the child is wrong and why they could get hurt, they simply snap and yell at them. Both sides feel hurt.

So when you get angry, ask yourself, "What am I thinking?" "Am I holding onto some fear?" If so, what is the fear, and how can you change it?

Anger can rear its ugly head in so many ways, such as envy. There was also a time I was angry seeing people I knew who were living the good life---professional friends living the life I wanted to live. I would find myself judging them. I wanted unconsciously for them to fail. I never wished ill will on someone but my jealously bred anger. I then turned it on myself. Why I couldn't achieve more? I knew I had to do something about my jealousy.

When I finally sat down to look at my anger, I realized I was just like my father. I was not living my purpose. I then thought, "What was my purpose?" The answer that came back was I wanted to be a speaker. I had a burning desire to create, but I had no outlet. When we are not dreaming, creating and growing — living up to our purpose on earth, then there is anger inside. No matter how old or how young we are, we all have a desire within us to create. It doesn't matter if it's creating a business, a painting, or artfully sweeping a floor. We are all creators. The question is, what do you want to create in your life? What are your dreams?

I had a desire to tell my story. I became a speaker, started a business, Self Awareness Trainings, giving workshops to thousands of people from teachers, entertainment industry groups, college students, executives, and law enforcement personnel. You name them; I have spoken to their group. I had to tell my story, especially by writing this book. The more I spoke to people, I realized the anger I carried dissipated, because I was living my dream. What is yours? Get busy and think about what you would like to do with your life.

## WHEN SOMEONE RUINS YOUR DAY

There are times in our lives when you are having a good day, then someone comes along and does something to upset you. Perhaps it was something someone said, or physically did to anger you. You may want to get back at them. But this only creates more suffering for you and for them. So what do you do?

## MINDFULNESS HEALS ANGER

Practice Mindfulness. We'll get into Mindfulness in Chapter 10. But just know it's a non-religious technique founded by Buddha to overcome suffering, and has helped millions for 2,500 years. It's now used in cancer, pain and stress management clinics around the country.

Phil Jackson is one of the most celebrated coaches in basketball today because he guided his teams in Chicago and Los Angeles to an astounding nine NBA championships. Jackson who calls himself a Zen Christian, (follows Christianity and Buddha's philosophy), shares with his players Buddha's teachings of the Noble Eightfold Path which includes Right thought, and Right concentration. This is being aware of what is going through your head, and making a decision to do the right thing. In his book, "More Than a Game," Jackson wrote, "Right thought means being in the moment as much as humanly possible."

So, when you are angry, try to tune into what you are feeling in your body. Notice your breath. Ask yourself, "What's going on inside me now?" Is your stomach tight? Do you feel blood tingling in your head? Are your muscles tight? Is your heart pounding?

When you tune into what your body is feeling, and notice your breathing, you can get control of your anger. But it's important when you are doing this, not to give yourself a story. Just observe the feeling of anger.

What helps a lot of people is when you tune into an anger reaction, to name the feeling. Say to yourself, "Pressure in head," or just simply, "Head." "Stomach turning." "Hands balled up in a fist."

You can do this while someone is talking to you angrily. You can be in control because Mindfulness helps you not to react to other people, but to act. To take the action that is needed to help you in that particular situation.

Buddha offered us a very simple exercise to become mindful of our anger by noticing our feelings and the inflow and out flow of our breath. Say to yourself, "Breathing in---I know I am breathing in. Breathing out---I know I am breathing out." And, you can shorten it to "Breathing in — breathing out." Shorten it more, "In — Out." While you are breathing in, you focus on your in breath, and you use the word, "In." The same with the out breath. Your mind may wander away from your breath many times. It does for everyone. Just bring your mind back and don't get upset. Try not to think of anything else but your breathing. Before long, you will find yourself calming down.

You can say "Breathing in, I feel angry, breathing out I release anger." Notice where you are holding anger in your body and name it to yourself, "Breathing in, head," "Breathing out I relax my body."

You can use this for fear, or any emotion that is overcoming you.

Mindfulness is especially helpful when you are dealing with parents and teachers, your boss, and other authority figures who may not be talking to you in the way you feel is right. But you know if you say something back, it will make it worse.

When people are talking to you in that manner, again, watch your breath. Say to yourself, "Breathing in I am angry, breathing out I am calm." This is a great way to comfort yourself when you are thinking about someone's actions that made you angry. Sitting in class, when you are lying in bed...or anywhere. Focusing on your breathing also improves your concentration.

When we ignore what's going on inside of ourselves, the energy builds. But when we look at our breathing, or the sensations of anger, we realize we are embracing anger. That alone calms us down so we can think straight. Prisons and jails are filled with people who let their anger run them. Often their reactions to someone who made them mad, was far worse than what the person did to them.

Mindfulness helps to calm your mind and your whole body. Most people simply lash out, or retaliate. If your life is being threatened, you may not have time to focus on what you are feeling. But most of the time we do. We get angry thinking about what someone did or said to us in the past. Take time, tune into your body and think about the actions you are about to take. Will it make things worse, or better? Non-violence is the best path to take.

## KNOW WHAT MAKES YOU MAD

Know your triggers. When you practice mindfulness, you can tune into what makes you angry. Most people don't know what makes them mad. But you can focus on your breath, and the sensations of anger; it helps you get real clear about not only anger, but everything.

There are certain things that upset all of us. Certain people, certain situations. It's important to notice these things especially if you find yourself continuously frustrated. If a person makes you angry, try to avoid them. But if they're people you simply can't avoid, maybe someone in your class, your teacher, or parents... observe your breathing, and the sensations of anger. This will help you defuse anger, and to think how you can make that relationship better.

## THINGS THAT MAKE YOU ANGRY

If it's a situation, like having to do a school assignment, notice that it makes you angry, but don't dwell on the fact. Denzel Washington tells his kids, "Do what you have to do, so you can do what you want to do." That means, if the work makes you angry, do it without all of the frustration and anger, so you can become a better person to be in a position to call your own shots in life. Observe your breath and the feelings that come up when you face doing the job and while you're doing what you have to do.

There are times schoolwork makes you angry because you don't know how to do the problems, or the assignment. Notice that anger, that frustration. Observe your breath, and then see yourself having completed whatever you need to do with a smile on your face. Then go look for help. Reach out and ask someone to help you or explain the work you have to do.

Again if you can't remove yourself from the situation, then you need to deal with it. This goes for anything you are facing.

## WHEN PEOPLE PUT YOU DOWN

One of the ways people feel superior, is by ignoring others. You may be the victim of this childish mind game. Before you make a judgment, ask yourself, if you're sure you have not done something to irritate that person. Could it be that someone else has told them something negative about you?

Regardless, you may want to take that person aside and talk to them. Maybe they are not intentionally ignoring you, perhaps they have just had a bad day. But if you think that person is playing a mind game, like pretending to be your friend in one situation, and ignoring you when they're with others, then know they're playing mind games, but you're not going to let them suck you into their "stuff."

They are lots of ways people try to put others down. They laugh at you when you've made a mistake in class; talk about you behind your back; make sarcastic comments about the clothes you wear; act like they know more than you; or just call you stupid. The list goes on and on.

Oscar De La Hoya, one of the most celebrated fighters in the history of boxing, remembers his classmates putting him down when he was in the sixth grade. "I wrote an essay about me wanted to be an Olympic Champion Boxer. Everyone started laughing," says Oscar. "It made me realize you have got to work hard to accomplish your dream—and that's what I did."

He has defeated more than a dozen world champions and won six world titles as well as an Olympic gold metal. Oscar has also been named in the 2008 United States Olympic Hall of Fame. Today he is also a businessman. Oscar formed Golden Boy Promotions, which makes him the first Hispanic to own a national boxing promotional firm and one of the only a handful of boxers in history who have taken on promotional responsibilities while still active as a boxer.

Instead of letting them make you angry with their actions, look at the situation differently. They obviously have some type of self-esteem issue or they wouldn't try to bring you down, to make themselves seem better. Maybe, they're simply jealous. You can make up a million reasons for them, but don't. You may never know. It's not important what they feel about you. What's important is how you feel about yourself.

Be sure and not take their actions personally, turn it in on yourself, and agree with what they are saying. What they say about you does not have to be your reality. I'll say it again, "What they say about you does not have to be your reality." What they say about you becomes real, only if you agree with them. Don't. Know they have the problem, not you. Focus on your breath, and how it makes you feel inside. Give yourself positive affirmations like: "I am a wonderful person", and "I believe in myself."

## EXERCISE TO RELEASE ANGER

Exercising is a great way to release anger. If you are not engaged in a team sport, the greatest exercise in the world to relieve anger is walking. You don't need special equipment to walk. You don't need anyone to do it with you, and you can do it in any types of weather, and anywhere.

## ACCEPT YOUR ANGER

Anger is a natural emotion. When you accept your anger, instead of trying to suppress it, you can get through that anger faster. When you suppress anger, you turn it in on yourself, and that only creates depression. Follow the Mindfulness steps on anger.

## SHARE YOUR FEELINGS

You can share your anger with the person who made you angry by trying to talk to them. But try to talk to that person in private. If that person doesn't want to talk to you in private, or there is not an opportunity, then you can resort to other things we talked about. But many times other people aren't aware they did or said something to hurt you, so try reaching out.

When you do reach out to share your anger with the person who made you angry, try to do it calmly, without attacking them. Most likely they will only attack back, and nothing is solved.

Talking to friends about your anger will help relieve the pressure. But be careful who you select to share your feelings with. Make sure that person will keep your feelings confidential and that they handle problems calmly. Reach out to adults; a parent, or a school counselor. There are also organizations who have people you can talk to.

## ORGANIZATIONS CAN HELP

My wife Janet was angry in high school when her mother and stepfather were constantly fighting because they both drank on the weekends. She found an Al-Anon/Alateen group.

For over 50 years, Al-Anon (which includes Alateen for younger members) has been offering hope and help to families and friends of alcoholics. It is estimated that each alcoholic affects the lives of at least four other people... alcoholism is truly a family disease. No matter what relationship you have with an alcoholic, whether they are still drinking or not, all who have been affected by someone else's drinking, can find solutions that lead you to peace in the Al-Anon/Alateen fellowship. These groups are also for people whose loved ones take drugs. If Al-Anon/Alateen is not available in your area, or this does not address your problem, try to find another organization you can contact for help like a church.

## SELF-TALK

A powerful technique athletes use to help them win games, is self-talk. Athletes talk to themselves all the time. Self-talk influences their emotions, mental pictures, physical states, and behavior. It can do the same for you.

When you are angry, you can tell yourself things like, "I'm angry, but I'm staying calm." "I know there is a perfect solution to this problem." "I am handling this situation in the right way." "What you think of me, is not my reality."

You can use self-talk when you are doing Mindful breathing. "Breathing in, I'm aware of my anger," "Breathing out, I calm my anger," "Breathing in I am aware of my thoughts, breathing out, I am in control of my anger." "Breathing in, I handle my anger. Breathing out, I am handling my anger."

We'll talk more about this in the following chapters.

## HANDLING ANGER WITH LAUGHTER

Laughter is one of the greatest healers for anger, stress, or most any situation. You can learn to look at anything in life with humor. But be careful not to use humor to put someone else down, especially yourself.

Humor helps defuse heated situations. I have used it many times when I found it hard to cope with pressures. I use it if I'm around someone negative, and it miraculously jolts them out of their mood, and makes them smile. It helps me dealing with those types of people too.

Some of the greatest comedians of our times including Chris Rock, Howie Mandel, George Lopez, Eddie Murphy, Dave Chapelle, Jim Carrey, and Jay Leno, all talk about how humor has helped them to deal with heavy situations, depressions, anger and other things.

Laughter helps you not to carry the heavy burden of anger. When you find people or situations annoying, try to make light of it and not turn your anger toward that person, or in on yourself. Your entire life, there will always be someone who will make you angry. So try to make light of the challenge, and roll with the punches.

## BE A LEADER, NOT A FOLLOWER

Ironically as I write this chapter I read this story, "A 15-year-old Temecula, California girl whose heart stopped during a fight among a group of teenagers was hospitalized Wednesday at Children's Hospital in San Diego."

I don't know what has happened, but you can be sure that whatever happened was what they call a "mob mentality." One person gets mad, tells a friend, they tell a friend, and before you know it a whole group gets worked up over something that was just between two people. Often what triggers these fights is something minor, or something disrespectful, or not really serious. This is also how gang warfare breaks out, and war among countries.

So be aware. If you are in a group, and anger surfaces about someone not in your group, are you going to be a part of that mentality, or are you going to be a leader and urge people to keep a calm head and think things through before reacting? If you can't, don't be afraid to walk away. Sometimes you won't be able to walk away. Or maybe you are afraid if you speak out people will label you as weak. This is when it's important to practice Mindfulness. Notice your breathing as people speak. It will keep you calm, and thinking straight, when others are worked up.

## REPLACE ANGER WITH FEEL-GOOD THOUGHTS AND ACTIVITIES

To help yourself get past anger, engage in activities that make you feel good. Leave alcohol and drugs alone. They may make you feel good for short time, but the consequences for indulging in these things only make your life worse. Instead, go to a show, look at a television program. Read something positive, or listen to music. Visualize a time in your life when you were really happy.

## FORGIVENESS

I believe a solution to channeling anger is forgiveness. Forgive others not because it's the nice thing to do, but because it sets you free from your anger. Anger often comes from holding onto things we have said and done in the past. The past is the past; there is nothing we can do about it. If there is something you can do to make it right with that person, then do it. Forget revenge, that will only make things worse. I mentioned this earlier, but it's worth repeating. If that person has moved on, died, or it would be opening up old wounds that you can't handle, write that person a letter. You don't have to mail it. But write it to get it off your chest.

One of the most important people to forgive is yourself. Often we carry anger because it's something we can't do, forgot to do, or won't do. Again, forgiving yourself is freeing yourself from the anger that keeps you stuck, and prevents you from being all that you aspire to become.

## JOURNAL

One of the most effective things you can do to help yourself through any negative emotion including fear, is to write about what you are feeling. This helps relieve the burden inside of you, and helps you to look at the problem in a new light. Journaling is especially wonderful if you can't find anyone to talk to about your anger.

## GET HELP IF YOU NEED IT

If you are feeling that you can't get your anger under control, and you want to hurt yourself, someone else, or animals, look for support. If you can't talk to your parents, try talking to a school counselor, or a spiritual leader in your community.

## DON'T LET ANGER HOLD YOU BACK

Holding onto anger not only keeps you chained to a bad situation, but it keeps you from moving forward in life. The world is filled with talented people who never realized their dreams because they are filled with anger and resentment. It reminds me of how elephants are trained for circus acts. When elephants are babies, they're tied to a stake in the ground with a huge thick chain. As time passes, the huge chain is replaced by a thinner chain. By the time the elephant is full-grown the trainers have replaced that chain with a simple rope. The elephant doesn't know it has the power to break free. That's the same with our anger. You have the power to break free of the chains of anger by releasing anger and focusing on your talents and gifts. When you do, you can move toward having the wonderful life you deserve, and your dreams will come true.

## RECAPS

1) What anger are you holding onto?
2) What gifts and talents do you have?
3) What would you like to become in life? If you don't know, read and try to find out what interests you.
4) Know what triggers your anger so you can avoid the situation.
5) Practice Mindfulness when you are angry. Focus on your breathing, and how anger feels in your body.
6) Exercise to release stress and anger.

7) Use self-talk like athletes, to talk yourself through a challenge.
8) Try to think of the good times you've had to neutralize your anger.
9) Try humor to defuse angry situations. Be sure you don't make fun of others, or you could worsen the problem.
10) Forgive to set yourself free. Write a letter of forgiveness even if the person has died. You don't have to give them the letter. The letter is to release yourself. Write a letter of forgiveness to yourself.
11) Be a leader, not a follower. Think for yourself.
12) Journal, to help put your anger in perspective.
13) If you feel you can't control your anger, reach out for help.

## AFFIRMATIONS

Today, I refuse to let my anger control me.

Today, I decide to create thoughts that bring me peace and happiness.

Today, I release anger and replace it with forgiveness.

Today, I remember that I am a positive, strong person, and I refuse negative thoughts of others.

Today, I am forgiving myself for_____.

Today, I have gifts that I am using to live my dream.

Today, I am right now developing my gifts.

## SPORT THE RIGHT ATTITUDE!

CHAPTER 7

# Using Setbacks and Obstacles to Win

"Winners never quit and quitters never win"

VINCENT THOMAS "VINCE" LOMBARDI
*Named "Coach of the Century" by ESPN*

EVERYONE ON THE planet will have to go through setbacks and obstacles in their lives. Some people will have more severe challenges than others. However, the one who can grow from and use their set-backs and obstacles, will always succeed. Obstacles can come in many forms; losing a game, failing a test, getting ill, or losing people we love.

Here are a few stories of great athletes who overcame their set-backs and obstacles:

## LANCE ARMSTRONG

World reknown cyclist Lance Armstrong has won the hearts of millions overcoming his setbacks. When he was at the top of his game he won the USPRO Championship title, stage victories in the Tour de France, A World Championship, multiple victories at the Tour du Pont, and a spot on the U.S. Olympic team.. In 1996 he entered as the No.1 ranked cyclist in the world , and competed as a member of the U.S. Cycling Team in the Atlanta Summer Olympic Games.

Lance had just signed a contract with the French-based Cofidis racing team when he received devastating news that would make many people not only quit racing, but quit life.

One day while cycling Lance was literally forced off his bike in excruciating pain. Doctors gave him the devastating news that he had cancer. It was advanced testicular cancer that had spread to his lungs and his brain. He had less than 50-50 chance of surviving.

Over time he was able to undergo treatment that worked, but while he was going through the pain and shock of cancer, it left him scarred physically and emotionally. Lance says now, "...it was the best thing that ever happened to me."

He knew he couldn't feel sorry for himself. He had to get back on his bike. This new way of looking at his setback helped him to see beyond cycling. He formed the Lance Armstrong Foundation to help others with cancer.

Lance finally recovered and returned to racing but he no longer had a contract with the Cofidis. He found himself without a team until the United States Postal Service took a leap of faith and signed him. He had to prove himself. But Lance was devastated again when he physically couldn't go on, and had to quit in the middle of race. People thought his career was definitely over.

It took time, but he learned to love the bike again and build up the courage to try again.

"Through my illness I learned rejection. I was written off," says Lance. "That was the moment I thought, Okay, game on. No prisoners. Everybody's going down."

Lance was determined not to give up. His new belief in himself and training, helped Lance finish in the top-five in the Tour of Spain and World Championships. In 1999 he set a goal for himself. The Tour de France. With strong determination, he won amazing victories, the 1999-2005 Tours de France.

How could Lance miraculously win over the odds? He believed he could beat the disease and win. "Pain is temporary," says Lance. "It may last a minute, or an hour, or a day, or a year, but eventually it will subside and something else will take its place. If I quit, however, it lasts forever."

## JEANETTE BOLDEN

Jeanette Bolden knows all too well about overcoming roadblocks. She won a Gold Medal for the 4x100 relay in the 1984 Olympics with an asthmatic condition. Today Jeanette is the 2008 Olympic coach of the U.S. Women's Track and Field team and the UCLA women's track and field head coach.

"I've had asthma all my life," says Jeanette. "Unfortunately, when I was young my mom used the Emergency Department as the primary source of treatment for my asthma. So I was in and out of the emergency rooms all the time and my asthma was really out of control. Things got so bad that I was actually sent to a home for asthmatic children, where I had to live for 9 months – away from my family. I did learn how to manage my asthma with the help of the people at the home, and learned to be much less afraid of it."

Not only did this extraordinary lady have to overcome her physical limitations, she had to deal with opposition from others as well. "I had problems with other kids picking on me because of my illness," says Jeanette. "I used to carry my inhaler in my sock and one time it fell out and a boy picked it up and started spraying it all over the place and shouting 'asthma face' and 'spasma girl' and he would tell others not to play with 'asthma girl.'"

When Jeanette returned from the home for asthmatic children, she resumed her life as a normal kid running and playing outdoors. One day she was with her younger sister at a park and they met a local track and field coach. Jeanette refusing to let her asthmatic condition hold her back, boldly asked the coach if she could join the team and explained that she had asthma. This was a gamble. She worried that he wouldn't want her on the team. But she was surprised when the coach simply said, "If it doesn't bother you, it doesn't bother me."

This was the beginning of her extraordinary life as a super-star athlete.

She got on the team, and never looked back even though she competed against healthy athletes with her condition.

"My mom always encouraged me to do my best and not let it (asthma) hinder me," says Jeanette. "Once I started winning races, my asthma became more acceptable. I don't think I would have accomplished as much in my career if I didn't have asthma – because it drove me to strive harder to prove myself to others and to show those kids who picked on me that nothing would stop me from excelling."

Not only has Jeanette refused to let asthma hold her back, she has embraced it and overcome the odds, and helps others to do the same. Today when she is not coaching, she helps others live a better quality of life with asthma as the founder and director of the Jeanette Bolden Asthma and Allergy Track Clinic. She is also a member of the Board of Directors for the Asthma and Allergy Foundation. Jeanette is the perfect example of the old adage, "When life hands you lemons, make lemonade."

## OSCAR DE LA HOYA

He has defeated more than a dozen world champions and won six world titles as well as an Olympic gold metal and has been named in the 2008 United States Olympic Hall of Fame. But Oscar De La Hoya would have never achieved his greatness if he gave up like he wanted to do when his beloved mother he was so close to died of cancer.

"My mother went to all of my fights even when she had breast cancer," remembers Oscar. "Sometimes she even missed her radiation treatments to support me. She didn't tell us she had cancer. She didn't want her kids to suffer.

"Her last words were for me to go to the Olympics and get the gold," says Oscar who remembers it was a lot of pressure on him because he desperately wanted to fulfill his mother's wishes...and at the same time, he wanted to quit boxing. "That pressure was incredible. I had to do it," says Oscar. "I learned I can go through fire in any situation in or out of the ring."

## MANNY RAMIREZ

Manny Ramirez, a 12-time All-Star Baseball Player, says his high school experience was complicated. When he arrived in New York from Santo Domingo, Dominican Republic he was never relaxed in class. He had no friends and Manny struggled learning English and fitting into a different culture.

"I was trying to learn to speak a different language... I always like to do things correctly, and it was difficult learning correct English, so I lost interest," says Manny. "This got me even deeper into baseball... When I played, I felt good about myself, because I could do my best. I could work hard and help our team to win."

Manny turned to his high school coach and talked for hours about what he needed to do to become an outstanding baseball player. Then he would turn the advice into practice. Manny would wake up at the crack of dawn to run before going to school, and after dinner he went to a friend's house to lift weights. He was a very hard worker. He never missed or arrived late to practice. He was the star of the high school team.

In 2008 Manny became a Los Angeles Dodger. He ranks 23rd on baseball's all-time home run list, and is one of only 11 players in baseball history with at least 11 seasons with 30 or more homers (1995-96, 1998-2006). He has also hit at least 20 home runs in 14 straight seasons, including a career-high 45 in 1998 with Cleveland and 2005 with Boston. Manny won two World Series championships with Boston in 2004 and 2007, and was named the World Series Most Valuable Player in 2004.

## MICHAEL JORDAN

Widely regarded as the greatest basketball player of all time, Michael Jordan suffered a devastating loss when his father was murdered in 1993. After three consecutive NBA titles with the Chicago Bulls, Michael quit basketball to pursue a lifelong dream to play baseball. Many felt the real reason he retired from basketball was his father's death.

In 1994 Michael signed a contract with the Chicago White Sox organization. He then spent the season with the Birmingham Barons of the Class AA Southern League—two levels below the major leagues. He played in the outfield and batted .202 with 3 home runs, 51 runs batted in, and 30 stolen bases. Later that year he batted .252 with the Scottsdale Scorpions in the Arizona Fall League. The Bulls, meanwhile, faltered without Michael Jordan. They won 55 games in the 1993-94 season but saw their run of three straight championships end with a loss to the New York Knicks in the Eastern Conference Semifinals.

In 1995 Michael Jordan was scheduled to advance to the Triple-A level with the Nashville Sounds of the American Association, with a chance to move up to the major leagues in September. But when major league players went on strike that spring, Michael Jordan decided to quit baseball rather than serve as a replacement player for the White Sox.

Michael ended his retirement from professional baseball by rejoining the Bulls with 17 games left in the 1994-95 season. The abrupt decision meant that Michael Jordan had little time to prepare for the rigors of postseason play, and the Bulls lost to the Orlando Magic in the Eastern Conference Semifinals. In 1995-96, Michael returned to his preretirement form, and he led his team to an NBA record 72-10 win-loss record during the regular season.

Michael has led the N.B.A. in scoring a record 10 times (1987-93, 1996-98), earned the M.V.P. award five times (1988, 1991-92, 1996, 1998), and won six championships with the Chicago Bulls (1991-93, 1996-98). Michael is called "Air Jordan" for his remarkable leaping ability thrilling spectators with his acrobatic dunks and game-winning shots. Off the court, Jordan became a celebrity and one of the most sought after commercial spokesmen in the world.

"I have missed more than 9,000 shots in my career," says Michael. I have lost almost 300 games. On 26 occasions I have been entrusted to take the game winning shot, and I missed. And I have failed over and over and over again in my life. And that is precisely why I succeed."

## MICHAEL PHELPS

Michael Phelps, who won the U.S. eight Gold Medals at the 2008 Beijing Olympic for swimming, has Attention Deficit Hyperactivity Disorder (ADHD). Symptoms of this condition include; not able to pay attention, makes careless mistakes, doesn't listen, doesn't finish tasks, does not follow directions, and is easily distracted. However, Michael broke through the odds with his laser attention that was so intense that some reporters called it "other-worldly."

The swimmer used hyper-focusing to bring home the Gold. This is a characteristic that ADHD people have, but usually they hyper-focus on everything that are distractions from the task at hand.

Michael believes he developed the ability to use what others consider an obstacle, ADHD hyper-focusing, because of the upstream battle he had to overcome as a kid being bullied. "I always had a baseball cap on riding the school bus, and some kids would take the hat, or throw it out the window, or my ears were flicked," said Michael in an interview with Bob Costas, host of the Olympics for NBC. "There was always something that I was picked on for, and I guess it made me stronger. All the stuff I had growing up, and all the making fun of (me), made me work harder to get to where I am now.

Today Michael uses people's pettiness to fuel his sport. "If there is trash-talking, it's extra fuel," says the Olympian. "Makes you want to prove that person wrong who says you can't do something."

Not too many people can trash talk Michael today. The 23-year-old is now considered one of world's greatest athletes.

## YOU ARE NOT ALONE

When we are going through pain and suffering, we often feel that no one else is living with the set-backs and are going through the obstacles that face us. This is not true. We may not know them, but everyone has their problems.

The key is that some people choose to change their attitudes and simply deal with their challenges like the athletes in this chapter. It's important to acknowledge your feelings, take time to grieve over a situation, then move on. Start by asking yourself, "How can I make the best out of this situation?" The answer will come to you.

## RECAPS

1) Set-backs and obstacles can make you stronger.
2) No matter what challenge you face, big or small, you can still win.
3) Inside each of us is greatness.
4) Never say never.
5) There is always someone going through more pain and suffering than you.
6) Your set-backs and obstacles can make you a better person.
7) Choose to learn from these challenges.
8) Ask yourself how you can move on.
9) Never, ever give up.

## AFFIRMATIONS

Today, I will make the best of this situation.
Today, I am learning from these challenges.
Today, I am becoming stronger and better.
Today, I am being led to solutions to my challenges.

## SPORT THE RIGHT ATTITUDE!

## CHAPTER 8

# Believe In Yourself

*"If you believe in yourself, have dedication and pride and never quit, you'll be a winner. The price of victory is high, but so are the rewards."*

PAUL WILLIAM "BEAR" BRYANT
*Legendary coach of the Alabama Crimson Tide football team*

THE YEARS OF family violence I was subjected to as a child, the sudden loss of my father, and the automobile accident all were so painful to me. I thought I would never be able to handle my pain, or ever feel good about myself.

Somehow I would have to pick myself up emotionally and believe in myself again. I decided I would use the principles I learned playing sports and apply these principles in my personal life to get moving forward once again.

A lot of people say, "As soon as my situation turns around, I'll cheer up and have a positive attitude." Or "When I see things change, I'll start believing I can be successful." But the truth is, we must believe in ourselves and sport the right attitude as we are going through the challenges. It's the law of attraction we hear so much about. Our thoughts of believing in ourselves create successes on and off the field.

If we lose focus of our purpose and start dwelling on the negative, it becomes easy to get disappointed and that disappointment can pose obstacles which prevent us from moving forward and staying committed to our vision and our goals.

All of us face disappointment from time to time and no matter how much faith we have or how good a person we are, or how hard we work, sooner or later someone will shake our faith, our belief in ourselves where we begin to say, "I can't do this." "It's too difficult," or, "I should just give up." This is the mentality that prevents us from believing in ourselves.

My wife and I founded a non-profit after school self-esteem and tutoring program for kids, and we called it, guess what? "Believe In Yourself, Inc." Why? Because we wanted the message to constantly be in young people's heads to believe in yourself even when they didn't. So when people asked them what they were doing after school, they would say, "I'm going to Believe In Yourself." It was a message not only for themselves, but also for others who heard the title. Believing is the most important thing you can do to become successful in life. No matter how much money you have, what race you are, where you live, what gender you are, all that matters is if you believe in yourself.

Michael Jordan, perhaps the greatest basketball player of all time said, "Obstacles don't have to stop you. If you run into a wall, don't turn around and give up. Figure out how to climb it, go through it, or work around it."

Arnold Schwarzenegger, the Governor of California, action film icon who is the most famous body-builder in the world, has that same "never-give-up" attitude, "When you go through hardships," says Schwarzenegger, "and decide not to surrender, that is strength. The mind is the limit. As long as the mind can envision the fact that you can do something, you can do it, as long as you really believe 100 percent."

Belief is one of the most important characteristics a player can possess during a game, especially if the outcome of the game is uncertain. When athletes are losing a game or any competition, even the most successful professionals experience doubts about themselves. Everyone feels this way sometime or another, but you have to keep believing in yourself despite the opposition.

On April 21, 2008 professional race car driver Danica Patrick became the first female IndyCar winner in history of the male-dominated sport. "You must believe in yourself," says Danica who doesn't doubt she could win a race. "No doubt, just a matter of when." If you believe winning is inevitable, then it will be for you.

The boxing movie "Rocky," struck a deep chord with audiences all over the world because we all have times in our life like the lead character when no one seems to believe in us. This is the time we have to believe in ourselves which is the inspirational moral of "Rocky."

Not only did "Rocky" win Academy Awards for Best Picture, Best Director, and Film Editing, but it was followed by five sequels, which inspired millions to "have faith in yourself no matter what odds you are facing." "I take rejection as someone blowing a bugle in my ear to wake me up and get going, rather than retreat."

In the movie, Rocky Balboa runs up the steps of the Philadelphia Art Museum as a triumph that he believes in himself. Today, thirty years after that film, the site has become one of the city's top tourist attractions. Bill Moore the museum's chief executive said, "We try to encourage people to actually go inside the Art Museum, too, but a lot of people just want to run up the steps."

Even the story behind the movie was about "believing in yourself." Sylvester Stallone is an actor who, at one time, couldn't get any roles, so he decided to write one for himself, which he did.... "Rocky." Then Stallone lived in a small run-down apartment, with only $106.00 in the bank. He wrote "Rocky" in three days and three nights. Stallone was offered $75,000.00 for his screenplay but he turned it down because the studio executives didn't want him to play the lead, but Stallone knew in his heart he was "Rocky." The actor held his own against powerful movie executives until they finally agreed to let him play "Rocky."

The actor became an American icon after playing "Rocky," and the results were incredible. But it was only because he believed in himself as an actor despite having a speech impediment that made him sound different, and having problems in school. "When I was in junior high school, the teachers voted me as the student most likely to end up in the electric chair," says Stallone . "I'm not handsome in the classical sense. The eyes droop, the mouth is crooked, the teeth aren't straight, the voice sounds like a mafioso pallbearer." Still Stallone had faith in himself and wrote these words for Rocky which he said in the film which inspired millions, "Believe in yourself, and you can do anything."

One my favorite sports is running. I love to run, and still do today. Running is truly about believing in yourself. If you don't, it will show up in how hard you train. You must believe in your ability or you won't commit to running better or faster. Those who don't believe in themselves will not train as hard, if it's for a marathon, 10k fundraiser, or a team.

Our body and minds are connected, so you can believe that you have hit the "wall" and can't run any further even if your body is capable of doing so. When you run, you can hit many psychological barriers that can stop you from running if you don't believe in yourself.

Roger Bannister believed he could break the record on the four-minute mile which had never been broken. Bannister believed he could and did. The same was said when New Zealand's John Walker believed he could run a mile in 3:50. — which he did. Now it's not uncommon to hear people running a mile in under four minutes. The point is, these guys believed in themselves and their abilities. Like Stallone, and the Rocky character, they believed in themselves when others didn't believe in them.

Are you letting someone else's doubts about you and your abilities hold you back? If so, refuse to be held back by yourself or others.

To begin to believe in ourselves, we first have to be honest and truly look at ourselves. We have to admit to ourselves that we don't believe in ourselves as much as we should, and that's OK. There is nothing wrong with feeling you don't believe in yourself. Many people feel that way around the world. Just use it as a starting point to change those thoughts that hold you back.

We can't change what we refuse to admit. Sometimes simply recognizing our weaknesses is the healing. Here are some ways athletes can tell if they are not believing in themselves.

Even if you don't play sports, these are still clues that you are not believing in yourself:

- a deep inner feeling of not being good enough
- extreme nervousness when you have to do something challenging like taking a test, performing or speaking in front of a audience, getting ready to play a game or meet
- negative thoughts of all types
- worrying about small details which may never occur. This is fear.
- intimidation from other competitors. People saying you can't do it.
- unusual or silly mistakes during a meet or game
- not looking forward to meets or games
- jealousy of other team mates. Feeling they are successful and you are not.
- jealous because your peers are willing to put in the extra work, and you're not

Now that you have identified traits of not believing in yourself, you can move on to turning those thoughts around to start believing in your success instead of failure. In the following chapters you will find ways champion athletes turn their lack of self confidence into believing in themselves...and you can too.

Jim Valvano coached nineteen years, including at Johns Hopkins, Bucknell, Iowa, and North Carolina State. Over that span, he compiled a 346-212 record and was twice voted NCAA coach of the year. His North Carolina State team won the 1983 NCAA Championship. Valvano died of lung cancer right after he received the Arthur Ashe Courage Award at the ESPY

Awards. He gave a moving speech at the ceremony which I, and millions of other fans, will always remember. He was passionate as he spoke these words: "In spite of problems, keep your dreams alive," says Valvano, "Don't give up. Don't ever give up."

## AFFIRMATIONS:

Today, I will be honest with myself. I will be courageous enough to admit if I don't believe in myself.

Today, I will try to find and talk to someone who can help me start believing in myself (Someone you respect and can talk to.) A parent? Relative? Coach? Teacher? Positive friend?

Today, I will begin to read positive things to help me believe in myself. (Check out books from the library, go Online and read about believing in yourself. Look at motivation and inspiration videos on YouTube.)

Today, I will carry a positive quote that will help me believe in myself.

Today, I will think of something positive about myself.

Today, I will believe in myself.

Here are some of my favorite quotes on believing in yourself:

*"I believe in me more than anything in this world"*

WILMA RUDOLPH, *Olympic gold medal runner*

*"You will never achieve anything great in life
unless you dare to believe that something inside you
is bigger than the circumstances you face."*

RUBEN GONZALEZ

*Three-time Olympian and National Luge Champion*

*"Some people say that I have an attitude - Maybe I do.
But I think that you have to. You have to believe in yourself
when no one else does - that makes you a winner right there."*

VENUS WILLIAMS, *world-class tennis champion*

*"Believe in yourself! Have faith in your abilities!
Without a humble but reasonable confidence in your
own powers you cannot be successful or happy."*

NORMAN VINCENT PEALE

*Author and world expert on achieving success and happiness*

*"If you believe in yourself and have dedication and pride –
and never quit, you'll be a winner.
The price of victory is high but so are the rewards."*

PAUL "BEAR" BRYANT, *legendary football coach*

*"To be a champ you have to believe in yourself when no one else will."*

Sugar Ray Robinson, *Boxing champion*

*"A man can be as great as he wants to be. If you believe in yourself and have the courage, the determination, the dedication, the competitive drive and if you are willing to sacrifice the little things in life and pay the price for the things that are worthwhile, it can be done."*

Vince Lombardi, named *"Coach of the Century" by ESPN*

*"People become really quite remarkable when they start thinking that they can do things. When they believe in themselves they have the first secret of success."*

Norman Vincent Peale

*One important key to success is self-confidence. An important key to self-confidence is preparation.*

Arthur Ashe

*One of the top ranked tennis players, and humanitarian*

*One of the things that my parents have taught me is never listen to other people's expectations. You should live your own life and live up to your own expectations, and those are the only things I really care about it.*

Tiger Woods

*Ranked Among the Most Successful Golfers of All Time*

CHAPTER 9

# Picture It In Your Mind: Visualization

*"Visualization is an important tool for me"*

PHIL JACKSON,

*One of the Most Successful Coaches in NBA History*

VISUALIZATION IS USING your imagination to create what you desire in life. Yet the term visualization can be misleading. Perhaps another word might be image---to put an image of something into your mind. Don't let the words confuse you, because either word is fine. Just see what you want.

I can remember when I was 10-years-old; I used to always create mental pictures of myself succeeding in sports. This started at an early age when I first became interested in sports.

Through these mental images I created, I knew that I could give extraordinary performances on a basketball court, football field, baseball field or track. I just felt that my talents were unlimited. I was like most young men who gravitated to sports. It was a way of expressing myself, as artists, musicians or writers might express themselves. Visualization was also a way to go deep down inside and touch that creative presence, which opened my imagination to ideas that could help me pursue my lifelong dreams.

A lot of times when I was growing up, I used to sit in our living room and play music that would help me create those mental images of what I wanted to become. I wanted to be a successful athlete.

When I created those pictures in my mind, I could feel a presence within me that reassured me and gave me a sense of confidence. It was as if the mental images were reality. I would let my total being melt into the music and imagine that the pictures were happening to me at that very moment.

The lyrics of certain songs expressed what I felt inside, and fostered in me a greater realization of success and the good things that could happen to me.

Had it not been for my accident I believe I would have surely achieved professional status. The scholarship offers from top colleges around the country and me constantly mentioned in the newspaper sports section, all pointed in that direction. But my accident took me in a different direction. Obviously, that was not the path I was supposed to take. I had to release my anger and focus my gifts elsewhere.

We can still be successful in whatever we choose even if we have to change directions. The important thing is not to give up seeing in your mind being successful.

When I became inducted into the Stockton, California, Black Sports Hall of Fame as an adult, I realized my ability to visualize myself successful, not only helped tremendously in sports, but also gave me the drive to pull through my accident. I transferred that same feeling of success to my present career as a speaker and author — which I love. Success is success no matter what you decide to become.

We can't all be superstar athletes, actors, singers, musicians...but we can be successful in our chosen fields. If you look at most any field, the successful people will most likely say they visualized themselves achieving their goals.

## HOW THEY DO IT

Successful athletes envision themselves winning in their sport. Coaches even draw pictures of the plays on blackboards in practice rooms. The diagrams show each individual player how he is supposed to execute his moves in order to make that play successful. Over and over again, athletes visualize themselves executing the right moves. They see themselves making the perfect block or pass to make the play exactly as it was designed on the board.

Phil Jackson believes in visualization. He guided the Lakers to three titles in his first stint as their head coach from 1999-2004, and guided the Chicago Bulls to six NBA championships in his nine years as head coach from 1989-1998. In his book, "Sacred Hoops," he wrote "Visualization is an important tool for me." Jackson helped his players not only visualize their success winning games, but he gave them guided meditations called, the "Safe Spot" during half times to help the players calm down to focus. The players in their visualization each went to a special place in their minds where they felt safe and at peace.

In 1968, two young football rookies, Art Shell and Gene Upshaw, became best friends when they met at the Oakland Raiders training camp. They would visualize their dreams and share them with one another. Upshaw hoped one day to be a politician, Shell wanted to be a football coach, and they both longed to be elected to the Football Hall of Fame.

By 1987, their dreams started becoming reality. Upshaw, who by then was the executive director of the NFL Players Association, was inducted into the Hall of Fame. The next year, it was Shell's turn. He became the NFL's first African American head coach in 64 years when he was named coach of the Los Angeles Raiders.

When Shell heard the news, he called Upshaw, who was elated, "I can't believe it, Gene," he said. "All those plans we made years ago have actually come true."

In his 15 seasons as a Raider player, 1968-82, Shell was named All-Pro three times and played in eight Pro Bowls, more than any other Raider ever. Like his friend Gene, he was also elected to the Hall of Fame.

The key to Shell and Upshaw's tremendous success was that they had pictures in their minds of what they wanted to become. They used their imaginations, worked hard, and dedicated themselves to creating an image of what they desired to manifest. Their dreams didn't materialize instantly, but they still continued to focus on those images and eventually they came true.

Jerry West, the former general manager of the Los Angeles Lakers, an extraordinary basketball player, as a kid growing up in West Virginia used to visualize being a basketball player. Jerry would dribble a ball on dirt well into the nights. His accomplishments have far exceeded his imagination.

"I was my own best friend," he says of those days, "I was everything, actually. Player, coach, announcer, even the time-keeper. It was amazing to me how many times in those imaginary games there would be one second left, my team one point down and me with the ball, and I'd miss and---the really amazing part---there would still be time for another, shot, or 10."

Not that many years later, and although the timekeeper was no longer his best friend, he would make a 60-foot shot at the buzzer to send a 1970 NBA championship game into overtime. Not even his dreams, as fevered as they may have been in Appalachian twilight, could have anticipated the glory of real life.

Every minute of every day we visualize, using the natural powers of our imagination to create certain things in our life consciously and unconsciously. We can see this principle at work. For instance, when we accidentally run into someone we've just been thinking of, or happen to find that book which contains exactly the information we need at that moment. But many of us have used visualization in negative ways rather than using it for positive growth. People frequently get angry because of what someone has done or said about them. Instead of forgiving and forgetting, they build on the negative, creating hurtful images of how they can get even. This is a waste of creative mental energy.

When we use negative mental pictures we develop an attitude which automatically attracts other difficulties to us. I had to work very hard to keep a positive frame of mind at my last 9-5 job. Constantly, there were situations where co-workers were talking about me and others behind our backs. Certain people in management were trying to make us employees feel less than important and our opinions were not taken seriously. This negativity about people and life causes us to imagine problems and trouble to be our way of life. There's a saying "You can't climb up the ladder if you are keeping your foot on someone else's hands who are trying to climb up too. You need both feet on the ladder rungs to climb to the top."

We are always using the natural powers of our imagination, but not always in useful ways. There is nothing new or unusual about using the mind and emotions as tools of consciously creating our reality. As we become aware and begin to eliminate negative visualization from our daily lives, we can begin to think and act in healthy, positive, affirming ways.

One of the great things about visualizations, is if you are going through tough times, and everything is negative around you, you can go into your secret place, or as Phil Jackson calls it your "Safe Spot" in your mind and see the life you want. You can create this whole world in your head that not only takes you out of negative problems...but leads you toward a wonderful future. No one can touch that special world but you. You can go as many times as you want.

Some people visualize a beautiful garden, and see themselves walking by a babbling creek. When you visualize try to put all of your senses into the process. For example, being in your garden, feel the soft wind on your face. Hear the birds, imagine feeling the warm sun — even imagine the smell of bright colored flowers. Ask yourself what kind of flowers are they. See wild life rabbits, squirrels. What color is their coat?

Some people have a hard time visualizing. If you are one of them, that's OK. Just try to get glimpses of what you want to visualize. Be kind and gentle with yourself. This may be new to you, and you are training your mind. Work on feeling the wind, or whatever you want in your images.

When you visualize, put all of your senses into the picture. Feel the end result of having achieved your victory. Ask yourself, "How would I feel if this came true?" Most likely you'll get a good feeling throughout your body. This is what you want to add to your visualization. When you feel and see something, your mind does not know what is true and what's not, so it will do all it can to make your dreams materialize.

It's important in your visualizations not to see harm coming to another person. Remember that what you put out, returns, especially when you visualize. See the power of the mind attracts what you think about. That's the great thing about visualizing. But if you are seeing hurt and misfortune come to another person because you don't like them, or want revenge, that same harm could come back to you because it's energy. Energy has a boomerang effect. So be careful what you wish for and visualize.

## ATHLETES VISUALIZE:

Jack Nicklaus also known as "The Golden Bear", and is widely regarded as one of the greatest professional golfers of all time, in large part because of his records in major championships, claims that his success is entirely owed to practicing concentration and visualization.

Mary Lou Retton is one of the greatest female US gymnastics. She was the first American to win the all-around gold medal in the Olympic Games in Los Angeles. *Time Magazine* reported in an Olympics cover story, "On the night before the finals in women's gymnastics, famous athlete, Mary Lou Retton, then age 16, lay in bed at the Olympic Village mentally rehearsing her performance ritual."

A 1984 survey of 235 Canadian Olympic athletes preparing for the Games found that 99 percent of them were using imagery. Professional athletes spend a good deal of time visualizing their victory by telling their minds exactly what they want their bodies to achieve. Timothy Gallwey author of "The Inner Game of Tennis" says, "Athletic improvement without the development of mental skills (such as visualization) is impossible."

There are many important aspects to visualization which you should know about (I could probably write 100 pages on this topic alone) so I will try to cover some of the important ones, plus special tips on how you can use visualization.

Craig Townsend Director of It's Mind over Matter in Sydney, Australia has worked with National and State level swimmers for over a decade, teaching them various methods of improvement through mental training. Townsend says the biggest problem he has found facing most swimmers is a lack of real belief in their own ability and knowing they can win or swim the time they desire. He says when these athletes lack real belief in themselves it creates fear which causes a variety of problems before races such as:

- a deep inner feeling of not being good enough
- extreme nervousness (which sometimes manifests as vomiting)
- negative thoughts of all types
- low energy
- worrying about small details which may never occur
- intimidation from other competitors
- unusual or silly mistakes during the race
- recurring problems
- not looking forward to meets/swims
- jealousy of other swimmers

Townsend says the best way to create belief in yourself and your own ability is to visualize every day for five minutes vividly imaging the perfect outcome. It helps program your subconscious mind for success, like a computer.

"When you visualize a race in your mind," Townsend tells swimmers, "Use all your senses - imagine seeing the swimmers, pool and surroundings in their respective colors, smell the chlorine of the pool, hear the sounds of people cheering you, and most of all - feel the joy of victory when you win the race or swim that time you desired. If you do this every day for around 5 minutes, you will gradually notice a shift in your confidence levels before races, and your times will begin to steadily come down." He says the benefits of visualizing everyday will help any one:

- overcome extreme nervousness
- reduce and erase pain
- learn new skills more easily and quickly e.g. kicks/turns
- overcome major intimidation from a competitor
- increase your energy
- relax more easily
- increase speed / reduce times
- banish negativity, and sustain positive attitude
- recover from illness and injuries more quickly

Shakti Gawain, a pioneer in the field of personal growth and visualization consciousness, says, "The most important thing to remember is to use creative visualization often, to make it a regular part of your life. Most people seem to find that it works best to practice it at least a little every day, especially when they are first learning." Albert Einstein said "Imagination is more important than science." Professional athletes have known this for decades.

## HOW TO VISUALIZE:

- Identify the goal you want to visualize. Find a comfortable place to sit and relax.
- Eliminate all distractions. Turn off the phone, television, etc. One of the best times to do this is just before you go to sleep, or when you wake up in the morning.
- Close your eyes and focus on feeling relaxed.
- Now, imagine yourself in the situation where you want to improve. Create a picture in your mind of the sights, sounds, and smells. You can picture yourself succeeding in sports, on a test in school, getting a job, or wherever you want improvement in your life.

- See yourself happy that you have attained what you wanted. How does that feel? See yourself smiling and happy after reaching your goal. Take a moment to feel the pleasure and excitement of achieving this goal already complete.
- Picture yourself finishing the course and feeling great, both physically and emotionally.
- Visualize a few minutes every day.

## AFFIRMATIONS

Today, I am easily and effortlessly seeing my goal accomplished.
Today, I see myself successful.
Today, I see myself___________________(your goal).

CHAPTER 10

# Coaching Your Thoughts

*"If you worried about falling off the bike, you would never get on"*

LANCE ARMSTRONG
*WORLD CHAMPION CYCLIST*

SUCCESSFUL ATHLETES IN all fields, swimmers, runners, skiers, and tennis players, football players, baseball and basketball players have a winning edge because they look at life differently. They believe in themselves and their abilities. Most athletes, coaches, and sports psychologists will say athletes have this confidence because they not only put the physical work into being the best, but because they mentally prepare themselves.

Many athletes mentally rehearse and prepare themselves before competitions. They visualize or imagine themselves already winning and they also do one more thing — self talk.

Self talk is a way of reprogramming our minds like computers. There is a phrase used by computer techies when computers were first developed, "garbage in, garbage out." We have to remember that when relating to our minds. Most of us engage in the wrong type of self talk. We put garbage into our minds by telling ourselves negative things like "I can't win," "I can't succeed because I'm not smart enough," "I'm not fast enough" or "I'm not special."

When I was recovering from my automobile accident, with multiple broken bones, and internal injuries, I also had to learn to walk again. I couldn't let my mind tell me that I would never walk even though I was frustrated and angry. It was hard work, my strength wasn't there, but I had to believe I would be back to top athletic form and the way I did it was with self talk and I imagined myself back on the field playing. I told myself constantly, throughout the day and at night that I was going to not only walk but play sports again. It took time, but I did and I made the junior college basketball team.

There are two kinds of self talk. Positive and negative. Unfortunately many of us engage in the negative self talk, constantly telling ourselves what is wrong about ourselves and our lives. Self talk and positive visualizations help us to reprogram our minds and take the garbage out.

Affirmations are simply a shorter version of self talk that are statements. Self talk and affirmations are a way of reprogramming our minds, like rebooting our computer that sometimes freezes when it gets a virus from spam. Negative self talk, doubt and fear are like the viruses of our minds. Our minds which are like computers, can easily freeze from fears and self doubts and never accomplish anything.

We have to reboot our minds just like we would do our computers with positive self talk and affirmations. Some athletes use phrases like: "I can do this." "I am good." "I can make it." "I am ready." "I am powerful." "I am successful."

Athletes are not the only ones who use self talk. Many people such as business people, and professionals in all careers, use positive self talk to help them reach their goals. These people not only give themselves self talk, but they also change their negative self talk. Before I talk about how to do self talk and affirmations, let's talk about dealing with negative self talk which many of us do constantly.

## NEGATIVE SELF TALK

Before positive self talk and affirmations can be effective, you may have to change the old self talk that has held you back. First be aware of the thoughts in your head. What are you telling yourself? Mental health experts differ on their answers but they say we have anywhere from 2,000-5,000 thoughts a day. They also say that most of our thoughts are the same, and most are negative thoughts. This kind of thinking not only creates failure, but lowers your self-esteem and creates stress as well.

Here are examples of negative self talk: "My life is awful." "Nothing goes right for me." "Everything is hard for me." "I can't do anything right." "I never get a break." "People don't like me." "I can't do this." "I'm not good enough." "This is too hard."

Being aware of the negative thoughts, which is also called being Mindful, is a powerful way to change negative thoughts. Mindfulness is awareness that acts like a laser to cut through those thoughts. (More on Mindfulness in the next chapter.)

Louise Hay, a pioneer in the self-help movement, and author of "You Can Heal Your Life," writes "Each negative belief that surfaces is a treasure. 'Ah ha! I have found you. You are the one that has been causing me all this trouble. Now I can eliminate you.'"

It's important if you are engaging in negative self talk, to not beat yourself up. Everyone has negative self talk, but we don't have to live with it. Successful athletes change it. But in order to change negative self talk, we have to tune into our thoughts. Most of the time the only thing we have to do is be aware of our self-defeating actions, and they fall away on their own, but here are other ways.

## HOW TO CHANGE NEGATIVE SELF TALK

**1. Avoid talk that leads to worry and fear.**

Not only do we tell ourselves that we can't do something, we tell others as well. So first stop saying what you can't do when you speak to others. You may not be able to change the thoughts you have yet, but you can control what comes out of your mouth.

**2. Avoid thinking about past failures**

If you've had past failures, and we all have, we don't have to wallow in our mistakes or things we couldn't accomplish. That's called living in the past. Try to correct the mistakes for the future then move on. Engage in positive activities to take your mind off of what has not worked in the past. Sometimes just listening to good music is a way to get your mind off failures. What are other positive activities you can do?

**3. Avoid "Stinking Thinking" about Yourself**

When you get ready to accomplish anything — sports, work, or school, and you think of yourself as a failure — that kind of stinking thinking influences the outcome of whatever you are trying to accomplish. You have already failed, because you said to yourself that you are a failure. So you don't have a chance of winning. Again, watch your self talk. Being aware of what you tell yourself is the biggest step in changing that habit.

**4. Avoid Fearing Losing**

Successful athletes avoid thoughts of constantly thinking about their opponent's wins; their reputation; their experience; and how many games or meets they have won. They review what they are up against, but they don't keep worrying about their opponents.

This tactic is important for anyone whether you are in school about to take a test, or at work dealing with co-workers. You can't worry about other people and how successful they may be because this holds you back with fear. That's why side blinders are put on racehorses to keep them from looking at the horses on their left or right. This way the racehorse can just focus on running the race. So can you.

**5. Think of your stress and fear in a positive way**

Everyone has stress and fear. It's often more intense when you are facing a competition, speaking in front of a crowd, or anything where you may be judged. But this type of anxiety is nature's way to help us prepare for whatever we are about to experience. The way to deal with these feelings of anxiety is again to be aware of them. Say to yourself, "I feel excited," "I feel shaky from nerves." "I feel fear." Notice where these feelings are in your body, and name where they are located, "head," "stomach," or "chest." Remember athletes feel this when they are about to go into a competition, like we all do when we are facing something big in our lives. Don't let this stop you from moving forward.

**6. Change Negative thoughts to Positive Ones**

When you tell yourself, "I am not going to fail," your mind pictures you failing at whatever you intend to accomplish. So instead, tell yourself, "I am winning," or "I am succeeding." The winning picture is the one you want in your head, not the one failing.

Remember successful athletes like Tiger Woods focus on driving the ball into the hole, instead of missing the swing.

## HOW TO CREATE POSITIVE SELF TALK USING AFFIRMATIONS

Some people think that if they say something positive when they are feeling negative, they are lying to themselves. But positive self talk or affirmations are simply re-training your mind. You are the coach telling your mind what to do. Athletes who are feeling doubtful about their abilities, constantly use positive self talk to talk themselves out of defeat.

Successful athletes not only give themselves self talk, they write down what they want to accomplish. It doesn't have to be a long. Boxing great Oscar De La Hoya wrote something short but powerful which foretold one of his highest achievements.

"I have always had big dreams. I always reach for the stars," says Oscar. "When I was 10 or 11 years old, I got an Olympic poster and signed my name to it." In 1992 Oscar won the United States' only boxing gold medal at the Summer Olympics in Barcelona, Spain.

This helps them to believe they can win, and their performances change instantly.

1. Write your affirmations as a positive statement. Examples:
   I am achieving my goals.
   I have determination and drive.
2. Read your affirmations daily.
3. Say or chant affirmations daily, for ten minutes.
4. Sing your affirmations.
5. Say your affirmations frequently.
6. Speak affirmations aloud to yourself.
7. Say your affirmations silently or aloud just before you go to sleep.
8. Use feeling when we you say your affirmations.
9. Draw your affirmations, and make them colorful.
10. Post your affirmations on your mirror, or wherever you look every day.
11. Say your affirmations in combination with your visualizations.
12. Write your affirmations 20 or 30 times.
13. Start your day by saying your affirmations with strong feelings.
12. To make your affirmations even more powerful, use spiritual references. For example: "I can do all things through Christ who strengthens me." "If God be for me, who can be against me?"(...or whatever your religious beliefs)

Affirmations and visualizations can produce positive changes in your life. Have fun creating them. Here are more affirmations:

## SELF ESTEEM

I deserve to be happy and successful.

I have the power to change myself.

I can forgive and understand others.

I can make my own choices and decisions.

I can choose happiness whenever I wish no matter what my circumstances.

I am flexible and open to change in every aspect of my life.

It is enough to have done my best.

I deserve to be loved.

I accept myself completely here and now.

I accept all my feelings as part of myself.

My positive thoughts bring me the benefits I desire.

Negative thoughts have no influence over me.

Everyday and in every way I am getting better and better.

I am confident and charming with the people I meet.

I radiate confidence and relaxation.

I start great conversations easily and effortlessly.

I approve of myself and feel great about myself.

I have sky-high self-esteem.

SPORT THE RIGHT ATTITUDE!

CHAPTER 11

# Focusing On the Game of Life

*"Meditation is not to escape from society, but to come back to ourselves and see what is going on. Once there is seeing, there must be acting. With mindfulness, we know what to do and what not to do to help."*

THICH NHAT HANH,
*International Peace Activist and Zen Master*

SUPER STAR ATHLETES must focus on winning competitions to stay at the top of their game. They must stay balanced, in control of their emotions, and calm. If you want to be successful in life, you too must do the same in the game of life as you work toward your goals. But it can be difficult to stay balanced and focused because of so many distractions. One way to overcome those things is to meditate.

Phil Jackson, one of the greatest coaches in the history of the National Basketball Association, teaches his players how to meditate to stay focused on the game. He is the Los Angeles Lakers coach and has led the Lakers to win three consecutive NBA titles, and as the head coach for the Chicago Bulls, led them to six NBA titles.

In his book, "Sacred Hoops," Jackson writes that being aware is more important than being smart. "For me, meditation is a tool that allows me to stay calm and centered (well, most of the time) during the stressful highs and lows of basketball and life outside the arena. During games I often get agitated by bad calls, but years of meditation practice have taught me how to find that still point within so that I can argue passionately with the refs without being overwhelmed by anger."

Meditation is often not easy, especially for beginners. It's a practice that must become a habit in your life. For that reason when I find that I can't sit down and quiet my mind, I practice Mindfulness, another form of meditation which Jackson teaches his players.

The advantage of Mindfulness is that players can use it in the middle of a game in an arena filled with fans who are screaming and yelling. Swimmers, golfers, skaters, and other athletes all practice Mindfulness whether they know it or not, when their minds are entirely focused on whatever sport they are practicing. Many call it being in the "zone."

Tony Dungy, head coach who led the Indianapolis Colts to Super Bowl victory, seems to live in the "zone." He's widely admired for his quiet strength on the sidelines, compared to other coaches yelling, stomping, and cursing at the players. It's no wonder his best-selling memoir is titled, "Quiet Strength: The Principles, Practices, & Priorities of a Winning Life."

Mindfulness, living in the moment, gives you quiet strength and peace over any obstacle. Dungy shared his practice dealing with the loss of his son who committed suicide. In a USA TODAY article (August 8, 2006, "Tragedy Forces Dungy to Live in the Present"), Dungy talked about his son's death, "...what it forces you to do is live in the present," says Dungy. "It's hard to do, but that's what you have to do. You have to program yourself to live in the present. Make the present as good as you can make it. Because you can't count on the future and you can't go back and redo the past." Mindfulness can help you through any tough times.

## WHAT IS MINDFULNESS?

Mindfulness is a non-religious Buddhist practice of being aware of your present moment. You are not judging, reflecting, or thinking. You are simply observing the moment in which you find yourself. When this happens, stress is released and you will find you are more alert and calmer.

This kind of meditation has been practiced for 2,500 years and it's a great way to release stress, improve concentration and help you become patient. Mindfulness is participating in any activity where you place your total attention. This is why many people feel relaxed when they are gardening, knitting, stroking their pets, watching fish in an aquarium, knitting, or doing carpentry. This is all practicing Mindfulness.

What I love about the practice is, you don't have to sit still, close your eyes and have total silence. You can practice Mindfulness standing in line in the supermarket, the bus stop, or wherever you are.

## HOW TO PRACTICE MINDFULNESS

There are many ways to practice Mindfulness. Here are a few ways that have helped me:

**Full Awareness Breathing**

Full awareness breathing sharpens our thinking, concentration, and helps us to develop wisdom. It helps our mind to stop wandering in confused, never-ending thoughts and gives us clear-thinking.

There are people who have no peace or joy because they cannot stop the endless mind-chatter. This pra tice helps us "to live in the present moment" ... to be here now.

Breath is the bridge which connects our body and mind. Athletes know they can calm themselves when they are facing competitions by doing deep breathing.

*Example:* Place your attention on your breath coming into your nostrils and follow it through out your body. Relax into the breath. To help you focus on your breath, you can lie down, place a book on your stomach and watch it go up and down.

**Label Your Breath**

*(try using all of the following, or find one that works for you, or make up your own)*

- Count your breath (Breathing in one, breathing out one, breathing in two, breathing out two...)
- Breathing in, breathing out" or "inhaling, exhaling"
- "In ... out"
- "Breathing in a long breath, I know I am breathing in a long breath. Breathing out a long breath, I know I am breathing out a long breath." (if your breath is short, label it "breathing in short breath.")
- Calm your body by saying, "Breathing in, I calm my thoughts, breathing out, I calm my thoughts."
- To help you concentrate, "Breathing in I concentrate my mind, breathing out, I concentrate my mind."

**Label Your Thoughts**

Labeling helps you to be aware of your thoughts. We suffer when we let our thoughts control us because we are not aware of what we are thinking.

*Situation:* Someone you do not like comes in the room.

*Your Mind says:* "I'm not going to speak to her today."

*Label:* "anger" or "anger thoughts are rising in me," or "having a thought I'm not going to speak to him today"

*Label:* Or softly say to yourself "anger, anger, anger."

## HOW TO BE MINDFUL OF FEELINGS

- Label the area in your body you feel discomfort, or sensation. Example: "head," or "whole body," or "neck," or "chest."
- Try to put your entire awareness in the center of that feeling and give it a label. Example: "sharp," "fluttering," "pressure," "pain," or whatever you feel in your body.

- Open up and surrender to the feeling. Don't be afraid. Say to yourself, "the feeling breezes past me, and I'm still here."
- Label what is happening with the feeling. Example: "moving," "disappearing" "staying," or whatever you feel. Example: Describe the emotion you are feeling in your body.

"A feeling of sadness has just risen inside of me."

"A feeling of joy has just risen in me."

"A feeling of anger has just risen in me."

If the feeling continues, continue to recognize it "A feeling of sadness is still in me." "A feeling of joy is still in me." "A feeling of anger is still in me." If the feeling of sadness is leaving you "A feeling of sadness is leaving me." "The feeling of joy is leaving me." "The feeling of anger is leaving me."

When negative thoughts or feelings come to you, don't try to get rid of them, they often become stronger. Just let them come up and notice them. Don't beat yourself up for having these thoughts and feelings, they are normal. Everyone has them.

Lastly, when you try to practice Mindfulness and any form of meditation, your mind will immediately try to distract you. You'll find yourself thinking, that it's too hard, or this is not going to help you. Just know that's the "monkey mind," and it's perfectly normal to have those thoughts. Try to stay with Mindfulness even if it's for a few minutes a day.

You can try letting one thing be your Mindfulness practice like brushing your teeth, taking a shower, or eating without turning on the television. Just observe how you feel doing these activities.

Remember, your awareness is the guard to the palace (your mind.)

## AFFIRMATIONS:

Today I easily and effortlessly practice Mindfulness.
Today I accept my thoughts and feelings.

## SPORT THE RIGHT ATTITUDE!

CHAPTER 12

# The Healing Powers: Love and Forgiveness

*"Family's first and that's what matters most. We realize that our love (for sister Venus) goes deeper than the tennis game."*

SERENA WILLIAMS
*Top-ranked tennis player in the world*
*and Olympic Gold Medal Winner*

WE MUST USE our power to choose love: not tomorrow, not next year, not when our circumstances get better, but right now. This is the most important choice we have. We need to be aware of its urgency.

In "Learning to Love Yourself," Sharon Wegscheider-Cruse stresses that love is essential for growth. However, many of us did not receive unconditional love in our childhoods. It was not clear to me that my ability to love and be loved had been impaired from problems in my childhood. I am not speaking of sexual lovemaking. I'm talking about the emotional love and support my wife wanted. It was difficult and even uncomfortable to verbally express this emotion.

I eventually realized that my resistance was rooted in my family violence. But it's a mistake to believe that my parents were totally responsible.

Negative patterns are repeated throughout generations of families. My parents did not openly share their love with one another. Therefore they had no open expression of love to pass down to their children. I would guess this is how it happened for them as children. They never volunteered to share their childhood with my siblings or me.

However, as a married adult, I could no longer hide behind my past, although I tried. I became a workaholic, always living for tomorrow, never having time to enjoy the moment, always chasing that rainbow.

One day my wife, Janet, said, "I want you to really listen with your whole self. You can make all the money in the world and have a mansion in Beverly Hills, but that still would not relieve my loneliness and unhappiness." When I heard that, I knew it was time to stop pretending that tomorrow would be better---after we got the new house, new car, more money, more money, and more money.

I was not the loving, understanding husband and friend that she wanted me to be. I had other worries on my mind as well. I was working as a full-time real-estate agent and we were still living in an apartment. A few of my friends who were also in the business had purchased beautiful homes and were making BIG money. My ego was telling me I had to keep up with the Joneses and that made me even more reluctant to change.

But when I looked at my wife as she struggled to control her tears, I realized how much I loved her and I knew I had to change. I thought, why do I keep putting us through this emotional pain? Why do I keep going through it? I got up and wrapped my arms around her.

The real-estate business made me so busy being busy, I had not realized our relationship had become as fragile as a snowflake and was quickly melting away. I had to fix what was broken between us, and there was not another day to spare.

My wife had always strongly believed that daily verbal interaction with her mate was a must. Together we pondered our situation for hours. We decided we wanted to register in Ernest Holmes College, the school of ministry and attend workshops dealing with relationships. It wasn't that I wanted to get involved with our church so much as I feared losing my wife. The next day we called the church and asked them to mail us a registration package. We became full-time students attending night classes for three-and–a-half years, while still working our full-time jobs. We also probably purchased and read every self-help book on the market.

I had to let go of my fears of being affectionate and surrender to Janet's love, but my ego was not ready to give up so easily. To reveal that side of myself, I had to give up my ego and become vulnerable to the feelings of love. I had to surrender to God and let God show me how to love. I prayed for direction. I was afraid to let go and love, afraid my wife would think I was weak and leave me.

When I accepted love's way, things happened. First, Janet became pregnant, after we had been married for six years. Our son was conceived out of love and not just lust.

We wanted a house, but I became frustrated because the area we wanted to live in was above our price range. I had made several offers on different properties but none were accepted. I slipped back into my old negative attitude again, frustrating my wife. We had disagreements, and anger but we were always civil toward one another. The one thing growing up in a violent home life taught me was to never, ever touch a woman in anger, and I never have. Janet, who had similar experiences in her childhood with family arguments and violence, would have left me if I even looked like I was going to touch her out of anger.

One Friday morning, I left for work. My wife had no plans to go in to her office, but had said nothing to me about it. When I arrived home that evening, there was a note saying she would call me in a few days. Motivated by a recent argument, she had taken our son and gone to San Diego. Our marriage was about to be over. I called her mother and our friends, and no one knew where she was. I asked God for direction and the strength to be more compassionate.

Meanwhile, I continued my search for a home. That Saturday morning, I headed North towards San Fernando Valley in Los Angeles county. We had always felt that because of the commute, the valley was not where we wanted to live, but this day I drove out there just to see what I could find. I ran upon a new development of homes for sale. The tract was developed in four phases and the fourth phase had been completed about a month earlier. They were all sold, except for one home that had just fallen through escrow and was back on the market. A two-story house with three bedrooms and a double–car garage, it was better than any we had seen before and more than we expected for our price range. I made an offer and 45 days later, escrow closed.

During that time, we had managed to work through our difficulties, and Janet returned back to me with our son. Communication is the key to any marriage. As we walked around in our new home, I saw my wife's happy face and realized I had to show my love. I needed to stop being self-centered and give to her emotionally, not only physically.

Love is thinking of more than just oneself. Love is thinking of others and their feelings.

Thinking of others is important in learning how we can communicate more effectively. When we do, we enable our relationships to operate at a higher level. Our past does not have to continue to interfere with our present peace of mind. Sure, the pain of our childhood may have contributed to our present behavior, but we don't have to remain stuck, which only prevents our life from moving forward.

The difficult relationships we sometimes have with our family, friends, and co-workers, are really opportunities for us to continually grow emotionally, socially, and spiritually. It's a time we can use to discover our real talents and gifts. Even, if your parents and other family members made you feel ashamed, insecure, bitter, and resentful, your happiness and peace of mind depend on your thoughts in the present. Try not to allow the angry thoughts about the past control you.

Have you ever noticed how uptight you feel when you are caught up in your family issues of the past? How your mind begins racing? One thought leads to another, and yet another, until you become increasingly agitated. Be mindful of what is happening in your head. Mindfulness, as we talked about in previous chapters, helps you to find peace over your thoughts, and prevents them from building up momentum. The sooner you see those negative thoughts before they start becoming mental snowballs, the quicker they dissolve. Remember just observing your thoughts is enough, you don't have to try to stop them. Mindfulness is powerful awareness that is like a laser cutting through those thoughts and emotions. Get into the practice of observing both your thoughts and what you are feeling without judgment, just watch. Be the witness.

There are times when you feel you can't be Mindful. You want to blow off steam. Think smart and find something constructive to do without letting negative emotions take over you making situations and relationships worse. This is an opportunity to let the athlete in you come out. Try doing some form of exercise. If you can't, or don't want to ... the best exercise in the world to blow off steam is walking.

Psychologist Carl Rogers coined the expression, "unconditional positive regard." The phrase means trying to accept people for who and what they are instead of criticizing them for being different from us. This is helpful to try to accept and forgive our parent(s) behavior for what happened to us during our childhood, even if they are not around. Forgiveness helps to reduce the stress of dealing with difficult family members and others.

Many times when we have suffered a troubled childhood we feel alone in life. This is a time to try to reach out to others who are worse off than ourselves. Mother Teresa even in her eighties, was ministering to the extreme poor and sick people on the streets of Calcutta. One day a reporter was scheduled to do an interview with her, and he followed her around on her mission. He was deeply touched and asked Mother Teresa if there was anything he could do to help her with her cause. "Could I help raise money or give you more publicity?"

Mother Teresa replied, "No, there is nothing that you need to do. My cause is not about publicity, and it is not about money. It is about something higher than that."

The reporter persisted, saying, "Isn't there anything else I can do for you? I feel so helpless."

Mother Teresa then said, "If you really want to do something, tomorrow morning get up at 4 AM., and go on the streets in your home town (he lived in Phoenix, Arizona). Find someone living there who believes that he/she is alone, and convince him or her that they are not. That is what you can do."

When we reach out to others and provide a helping hand, we realize there are people who have experiences that are worse than ours. This helps us to see we are not alone. Helping others allows us to put our problems behind us, and to find the good in our lives.

I remember times in my life feeling very alone because of the troubles growing up in a violent family. But sometimes helping the people closest to us who have at one time caused us pain, is a way of healing.

For years I carried anger, and my mother and I didn't get along. I never quite forgave her for not leaving my father because of all the pain he caused our family.

When I became an adult, my mother got sick with cancer, and I was the only one of her children who cared for her. A few years earlier, my sister passed away at the prime of her life suddenly from a brain aneurysm. She was one step away from becoming the first female warden at a California prison. My brother lived in a different state. So when I was unable to convince mom to move to Los Angeles, I made frequent 500-mile trips to care for her. There were several times when she didn't have anyone to take her to the doctor, or she refused to take a cab, I got on the road at 2:30AM so that I could drive to Stockton in time to take her to 9:30am doctor's appointment. I then in the same day, returned to Los Angeles because I couldn't stay the night. On these long, lonely road trips, I had plenty of opportunity to think about the past and work on forgiving my mother.

Going back to Stockton, I had to face all of the old emotions that haunted me. I had left there when I graduated from college. But now I had to face everything I left behind. I realized these were lessons I had to learn going back there. I had to learn how to forgive her, and how to love who she was.

I also had to let go of the accident that left me resentful and filled with anger that carried over into my adult life. Going back home and helping her through her illness, brought all of those emotions up again for me to look at and heal.

Being face to face with my mother, having her depend on me, made me realize that the anger and frustrations I carried may not have only been because of the family violence, but my accident as well.

The last days of mom's life suddenly became the best and most beautiful of our relationship. We still bickered, but we also talked and even laughed about the past. Slowly I realized that all of the violence I experienced between her and dad, I had held onto all of those years. I didn't know that I had this resentment toward her for not leaving my father. But now I realized it was something I had to let go.

I had to forgive her, and my father who had long ago died at the hands of a stranger. He was gone, but I had to forgive him for the things he did to mom, and for suddenly leaving me by dying.

While taking mom to doctors driving the familiar streets I was amazed at how the town had grown to a population of 250,000. When I lived there it was only 50,000 people. I realized that I didn't leave Stockton, I had run from the city and from my past. Even when I returned in 2001 to be inducted into the Black Sports Hall of Fame, I came just in time for the ceremony and left the next day.

Now helping mom, I was forced to stay awhile and make peace with that part of my life I left behind...or so I thought.

It taught me that even when we have weathered the most difficult times, the memories of past pains still linger, and that they are opportunities to be a mental athlete. We can learn from those losses and upsets, and get back in the game of life and sport the right attitude.

When I laid mom to rest in March, 2005, I stood over her grave with a clear conscience and a light heart. She had done the best she could with a fifth-grade education. I had forgiven her during the last days of her life, and truly showed her how much I loved her before it was too late.

Who in your life do you need to forgive before it's too late? Even if they have passed on like my father, you can still forgive them. You'll find when you do, it's like a huge boulder rolling off your chest freeing you to see the lessons you can learn. These are life lessons that today can help you too. Sport the Right Attitude.

## RECAP:

- Who can you show more love to in your life?
- Who can you forgive?
- Is there something you can forgive about yourself?

## AFFIRMATIONS

Today, I will live in present, and not keep dwelling on my past mistakes.

Today, I will forgive others.

Today, I will love myself.

## SPORT THE RIGHT ATTITUDE!

# Bibliography


Beattie, Melody. Codependent No More. New York: Harper & Row, 1987

Berne, Eric. Games People Play. New York: Grove press, 1973.

Black, Claudia. It Will Never Happen To Me. Denver, Colorado,: M.A.C., 1982

Bradshaw, John. The Family. Deer Beach, FL: Health Communication, 1988

Brigg, Corkille Dorothy. Celebrate Your Self. NY: Doubleday & Co., 1977.

Carnegie, Dale. How to Develop Self-Confidence And Influence People By Public Speaking Mass Market Paperback 1991

Cousins, Norman. Anatomy of an Illness. New York: Bantam Books, 1979

Dungy, Tony Quiet Strength:The Principles, Practices, & Priorities of a Winning Life Tyndale Publishers, Inc., 2007

Dyer, Wayne Your Erroneous Zones. New York: Funk and Wagnalls, 1976

Gallwey, Timothy The Inner Game of Tennis. Random House Publishing, 1974

Goldsmith, Joel S. Practicing the Presence. New York: Harper and Row, 1952

Helmstetter, Shad. The Self-Talk Solution. New York: Pocket Books, 1987

Jackson, Phil. Sacred Hoops: Spiritual Lessons of a Hardwood Warrior. 2006

Maltz, Maxwell. Psycho-Cybernetics. Los Angeles, Ca. Wilshire Book Co., 1960

Nhat Hahn, Thich. The Miracle of Mindfulness, Beacon Press, 1999

Satir, Virgina. The Satir Model. Palo Alto, California, Science and Behavior Books, Inc., 1991.

Seabury, David. Stop Being Afraid. Los Angeles, Calif. Science of Mind Publications, 1965
De La Hoya, Oscar, American Son, HarperCollins Publishers, 2008
Hay, Louise, You Can Heal Your Life, Hay House Publishing, 1999

# Index

# About the Author

WALTER JACKSON, MSC.D. is a behavioral consultant and personal growth expert, who has been a guest on public television shows, and radio talk shows around the country. Since 1993 he has facilitated effective communication workshops to thousands with his wife Janet, for teachers, parents, youth, and members of law enforcement, health care, corporate world and the entertainment industry. Walter began his work reaching out to young adults as a juvenile probation officer. He is co-founder and former CEO of Believe in Yourself, Inc., a non-profit self-esteem and tutoring program for elementary school children and their parents Walter earned his bachelor's in Social Work at California State University, Sacramento. He attended the ministry at Ernest Holmes College, and earned his Metaphysical Doctorate from the University of Metaphysics. He was also an advisor for the California State Prison.

In 2001 Walter was inducted into the Black Sports Hall of Fame in Stockton, California where he was born and raised. He is the father of three, and lives in Los Angeles with his wife Janet, an author of "A Cry for Light: A Journey into Love."

For more information about Walter's workshops and speeches:

Contact:
Self Awareness Trainings, LLC
645 West 9th Street, Unit 110
Los Angeles, California 90015-1640
Los Angeles, California 90027

info@SportingtheRightAttitude.com
and phone number 818-899-8812

Visit Walter's website:
www.SportingtheRightAttitude.com